THE HERMIT
IN THE GARDEN

Oxford University Press publications by Gordon Campbell

AS AUTHOR

The Oxford Dictionary of the Renaissance
Renaissance Art and Architecture
John Milton: Life, Work and Thought (co-author)
Milton and the Manuscript of 'De Doctrina Christiana' (co-author)
Very Interesting People: John Milton
Bible: The Story of the King James Version, 1611–2011

AS EDITOR

The Holy Bible: Quatercentenary Edition
The Grove Encyclopedia of Decorative Arts (2 vols.)
The Grove Encyclopedia of Classical Art and Architecture (2 vols.)
The Grove Encyclopedia of Northern Renaissance Art (3 vols.)
Renaissance Studies (10 vols.)
The Review of English Studies (13 vols.)
The Complete Works of John Milton (11 vols., in progress)
W. R. Parker, *Milton: A Biography* (2 vols.)
Ben Jonson, *The Alchemist and other Plays*

AS CONTRIBUTOR

Grove Art Online
John Bunyan: Conventicle and Parnassus
John Milton: Life, Writing, Reputation
The Journal of Theological Studies
The Oxford Chronology of English Literature
The Oxford Companion to English Literature
The Oxford Companion to the Garden
The Oxford Dictionary of National Biography
The Oxford Handbook of Milton

The HERMIT in the GARDEN

From Imperial Rome to Ornamental Gnome

GORDON CAMPBELL

OXFORD
UNIVERSITY PRESS

OXFORD

UNIVERSITY PRESS

Great Clarendon Street, Oxford, OX2 6DP,
United Kingdom

Oxford University Press is a department of the University of Oxford.
It furthers the University's objective of excellence in research, scholarship,
and education by publishing worldwide. Oxford is a registered trade mark of
Oxford University Press in the UK and in certain other countries

First Edition published in 2013

Impression: 1

British Library Cataloguing in Publication Data

Data available

ISBN 978–0–19–969699–4

Printed in Great Britain by
Clays Ltd. St Ives plc

PREFACE

Forty years ago I was living in York, writing a thesis on John Milton. I had a tiny hermit's cell in the university library, from which I could forage in the forest of books around me. I knew that long after his death Milton's body had been dug up and parts of it sold, and one day I decided to read Edith Sitwell's essay on the subject ('On the benefits of posthumous fame'), which was included in her *English Eccentrics: A Gallery of Weird and Wonderful Men and Women*, first published in 1933. As I scanned the contents page for the Milton essay, my eye lit on another, called 'Ancients and Ornamental Hermits'. The idea of keeping an ornamental hermit in one's garden was entirely new to me (as it will be to many readers of this book), and I was captivated. The publication of this book represents my release from that long captivity.

The revolution in garden design in eighteenth-century England brought follies into landscape gardens, and these follies often included hermitages. In some circles it was deemed desirable to hire a hermit to live in one's hermitage. These were not religious figures, but rather secular hermits. They were figures in the landscape, but their existence reflected a serious vein in Georgian culture. Who were these people? Why did landowners think it appropriate to have them in their gardens? What function did they serve? Why did some landowners style themselves hermits? Why did others build hermitages with imagined hermits who had perpetually stepped out for a moment? Where are these hermitages, and what do they look like? These are the questions that prompted the research that underpins this book.

The documentary foundation for the study of ornamental hermits is disconcertingly sandy. The essay by Edith Sitwell that drew me into the subject was largely derivative, in that much of her material was drawn from John Timbs's chapter on 'Hermits and the Eremetical Life' in his *English Eccentrics and Eccentricities* (1875). Timbs's chapter was in turn also largely derivative, in that he took some of his core material from an essay by 'Florence' on 'Hermits, Ornamental and Experimental', in *Notes and Queries* (1852). 'Florence' cites sources, but the material that he quotes is elusive. Is he reliable? And who was he?

There has never been a book solely devoted to ornamental hermits and their hermitages, so there are no familiar tram tracks for me to follow. In constructing my own tracks, I have chosen to begin with a small house at Hadrian's villa near Rome and range through subjects from Adam's hut in Eden and a chapter in a novel by Rousseau to the retirement home of an American president and the palace of a Russian empress. The paths that connect the hermits and their hermitages do not follow the geometrical contours of Renaissance gardens, but rather resemble the winding paths of the mid-eighteenth century, the period when the fashion for garden hermitages was at its height. Readers who choose to follow these paths will have many occasions on which to pause for moments of pleasing melancholy. The paths are not strewn with footnotes, which are melancholic without being pleasurable, but I have appended a list of hermitages and full list of works consulted to enable the curious reader to pursue any brambled byways that arouse interest. I have tracked down as many hermits and hermitages as I could, but every foray into eighteenth-century correspondence seems to bring yet another hermitage to light, and the process could go on indefinitely. I have therefore decided to call a halt, and to declare myself content to hear from any reader who knows of a Georgian hermit or hermitage that I have overlooked.

ACKNOWLEDGEMENTS

I have spent most of my professional life in a tower at the University of Leicester, ensconced in an elevated hermit's cell with a view. Like Simeon Stylites on his pillar (in Gibbon's account), I have 'resisted the heat of thirty summers, and the cold of as many winters', and enjoyed the company of many visitors who have climbed the tower expecting to be taught. I have also been reading in my tower, and in connection with this project have particularly benefited from the published version of an important lecture on garden hermitages delivered long ago by John Dixon Hunt. It was Professor Hunt, then a young lecturer in English, who first interested me in garden history; he has since gone on to shape the discipline of garden history, of which he is now the *doyen*. I have also learnt much from the researches of Eileen Harris, published in essays in *Country Life* and in an edition of Thomas Wright's *Universal Architecture*. Of more recent essays, I would single out one by Edward Harwood, who offers a historically situated account of the significance of the hermit in eighteenth- and nineteenth-century culture. I have drawn extensively on excellent reference books, notably Barbara Jones's *Follies and Grottoes* and James Howley's *Follies and Garden Buildings of Ireland*. The solid scholarship of Timothy Mowl's 'Historic Gardens of England' series (12 volumes to date) is a wonderful resource from which I have often benefited. Electronic assistance has come from a multitude of sources, but I am particularly grateful for the databases of listed buildings in England, Ireland and Scotland, and for the vast amount of reliable material in *Oxford Art Online* and in the *Oxford Dictionary of National Biography*.

Writing in this aerial hermitage is consistent with the eremetical ideal of the *vita contemplativa*, but research on ornamental hermits and their hermitages inevitably necessitates participation in the *vita activa*, in that I have had to journey far from my eyrie in search of hermitages in England, Scotland, and Ireland. Landowners have (with a single exception) allowed me to visit their hermitages, and I am grateful for their cordiality and kindness. My companion (and photographer) on these journeys has been my wife Mary, who has patiently lived with my writing projects for decades, but has never had to deal with one quite as Pythonesque as ornamental hermits. On this occasion she also read the entire text in draft, pruning some of its wilder excesses and sillier slips. Other assistance has been afforded by Frances Austin-Jones (on Stourhead), Lord Ballyedmond (on Ballyedmond), Stephen Barker (on Vauxhall), Alicia Black (on *Notes and Queries*), Sue Blaxland (on Painshill), Richard Bonney (on French hermitages), Kirsten Campbell (on Gaillon), Stuart Campbell (on Eastbourne), Jan Clark (on Painshill), Anne Marie D'Arcy (on Osbert Sitwell), Balz Engler (on Arlesheim), Stella Fletcher (on religious hermits), Susan Frost (on Selborne), Elizabeth Goldring (on Woodstock), Sandy Haynes (on Enville), Ian Jackson (on 'Florence'), The Very Revd Robert Jeffery (on Tong), The Knight of Glin† (on Glin Castle), Sarah Knight (on Theobalds), Stella Lanham (on Alison Lurie), Mary Ann Lund (on J. I. M. Stewart), Alan Power (on Stourhead), Sir William and Lady Proby (on Elton Hall), Antony Ravenscroft (on The Leasowes), Joanne Shattock (on nineteenth-century periodicals), Cathryn Spence (on Jeremiah Peirce and Thomas Robins), Oliver Stanley (on the Lilliput landscape and hermitage), Anna Swärdh (on F. M. Piper), Roger Warren (on Guy's Cliffe), and Janet Wheatcroft (on Craigieburn).

Oxford University Press has provided the tools and the people that have made this book happen. The book was commissioned by Luciana O'Flaherty, who cheerfully exceeded the editorial ideal of reading a draft of the book by reading two drafts; in the course of these readings she made many shrewd suggestions, all of which I have gratefully implemented. The process of coaxing the project from contract to submission fell to Matthew Cotton, who kept many balls in the air as we negotiated a complex series of obstacles. Production was overseen by Emma Barber, picture research was conducted by Deborah Protheroe, copy-editing by Dorothy McCarthy, text design by Jonathan Bargus, and proof-reading by Hayley Buckley. Marketing and publicity were organized by Emily Crowley-Wroe, Rosanne Dawkins, Phil Henderson, and Anna Silva in Oxford, and Christian Purdy and Elyse Turr in New York. The index was prepared by Gillian Northcott, with whom I have worked on many books. Enthusiastic support was offered from senior management by Sophie Goldsworthy. The two anonymous readers for OUP were formidably competent and immensely helpful. I wish that I could thank them by name, because they are in significant part responsible for the contours of the book, and they saved me from many foolish errors.

G.C.

Leicester 2013

CONTENTS

LIST OF COLOUR PLATES

LIST OF ILLUSTRATIONS

1

Origins and Antecedents

A guide to Hawkstone, the Shropshire estate of Sir Richard Hill, appeared in its second edition in 1784. This slim volume contained a description of the estate's resident hermit (a 'solitary sire') and his

> well-designed little cottage, which is an hermit's summer residence. You pull a bell, and gain admittance. The hermit is generally in a sitting posture, with a table before him, on which is a skull, the emblem of mortality, an hour-glass, a book and a pair of spectacles. The venerable bare-footed Father, whose name is Francis, (if awake) always rises up at the approach of strangers. He seems about 90 years of age, yet has all his senses to admiration. He is tolerably conversant, and far from being unpolite.

At the age of 90, Father Francis could not be expected to be perpetually on duty, and so was from time to time replaced by a stuffed hermit dressed as a druid and able to move and speak. Visitors to Hawkstone delighted in the hermit, but did not think it surprising to find such a person living in the grounds of an estate. The phenomenon of the ornamental hermit living in the garden strikes the twenty-first-century reader as bizarre, even hilarious, but in the eighteenth century it was for the most part taken seriously. There were detractors, but many visitors to gardens respected the figure of the hermit as an embodiment of the ideals of solitary retirement and pleasing melancholy. This chapter begins the quest to understand the phenomenon of the hermit in the garden through an examination of its origins.

The garden hermitage and its resident ornamental hermit is sometimes said to have emerged suddenly in the second quarter of the eighteenth century. There is a limited sense in which this is true, in that the ideology of the Georgian hermitage is peculiar to that period, but both the secular hermit and the secular hermitage have important precedents, of which I distinguish four: religious hermits in gardens, secular court hermitages, Elizabethan garden buildings, and earlier British hermits.

The religious hermit in the garden

The golden age of real hermits, people who withdrew into solitude for religious motives, extended from late antiquity until the Counter-Reformation of the sixteenth century. Thereafter in the western church the ideals of the eremetical life lived on in attenuated form, notably in monastic orders such as the Carthusians and the Carmelites. The enclosed communities of the church sometimes accommodated hermits, as did the enclosed gardens of the aristocracy.

The idea of the hermit in the garden has its origins in southern Europe, but precisely where is unknown. Renaissance Italy seems likely, but there are neither survivals nor documents to demonstrate such connections. One possible link between these putative Italian origins and France, where the first garden hermits appeared, would be the hermit Francesco di Paola (founder of the Minim Friars), who as a young man had lived in caves in southern Italy (including one on his father's estate), and in 1483 had gone to Plessis-les-Tours to attend the dying king, and stayed there for the rest of his life. He acquired a sort of celebrity status, and it is not unlikely that this model of the king's hermit was influential. At Vieil-Hesdin (now a village, but once a substantial town), in what is now northern France, the dukes of Burgundy had a retreat (destroyed by the army of Charles V in 1553) with a small house for the duke with a nearby cell and chapel for a hermit. At Chantilly, to the north of Paris, clergy in the chapels in the park included a hermit who was permitted to grant indulgences; whether he was resident in the park is not clear.

The earliest garden with a well-documented hermitage is near Rouen, in northern France. It is the garden of Château de Gaillon, the first Renaissance château in France. The château was built by Cardinal Georges d'Amboise, archbishop of Rouen and minister of King Louis XII, and was designed to serve as his summer archiepiscopal residence. Construction began in 1502, and in the same year the cardinal-archbishop commissioned the Italian priest and garden designer Pacello da Mercogliano to lay out the gardens. Within these gardens there was a private retreat called Le Lydieu, which contained a small house, a chapel, a small garden, and the first garden hermitage in France.

In the 1550s Charles Cardinal de Bourbon decided to aggrandize this part of the garden in imitation of similar gardens built by Italian princes of the church. The small house became a sumptuous two-storey white marble pavilion called the Maison Blanche, which was set on an island at one end of a short canal dug for the purpose. At the other end of the canal a rockwork hermitage was constructed on an island in a large water tank. This reconfigured part of the garden is pictured in two engravings by Jacques Androuet du Cerceau the elder, and it is possible that he was the designer, but his account of the hermitage has a detachment that may imply that he was describing someone else's work:

> You walk from the upper garden through the park . . . and you arrive at a little chapel and house and hermit's rock in the middle of a square basin of water. . . . To get there you cross a swing bridge, close by a little garden with statues three or four feet high, mounted on a plinth, depicting allegorical subjects; there are also several arbours [*berceaux*] covered with greenery. The hermitage is as beautiful and alluring and charming as any that you will find elsewhere.

The proprietors of Gaillon were cardinals, but this architectural ensemble is almost wholly secular. The pavilion is designed as a miniature château, and the rockwork hermitage also seems to be the realization of an architect's design. The Cardinal de Bourbon dubbed it 'La Parnasse de Gaillon', so declaring lightheartedly that its origins lay in the classical Parnassus, the limestone mountain on whose slopes lay the Corycian Cave that was home to Pan and the muses. It was a splendid hermitage, but there is no evidence that there was ever a hermit; it did, however, have a small chapel, but the religious use for which this building was intended is unknown.

The hermitage at Gaillon was not to have progeny in France, but there may be a link with one in the Bratislava residence of György Lippay, archbishop of Esztergom (Slovakia was then part of Hungary). From 1642 to 1663 Lippay remodelled the garden of this summer palace (Letný arcibiskupský palác) in a late Renaissance style. Its features included a Mount Parnassus decorated with classical statues, and a 'ruined' hermitage decorated with statues of saints. The garden is now lost (overlaid by an 'English garden'), except for an equestrian statue of St George. As with Gaillon, it is not known whether the hermitage had a religious function.

Claims are sometimes advanced that Gaillon influenced the garden hermitages of Spain. This is possible, but it is more likely that the garden hermitage in Spain was a separate development, possibly drawn from a common Italian antecedent.

The origin of the garden hermitage in seventeenth-century Spain can be traced to the previous century, when the emperor Charles V decided to spend his final years in eremetical seclusion at the Hieronymite monastery of Yuste (in Estremadura, central Spain), to which he withdrew in 1556, having abdicated as duke of Burgundy (i.e. ruler of the Netherlands), king of Naples (i.e. ruler of southern Italy), Holy Roman Emperor (i.e. ruler of the Habsburg lands, including Germany) and king of Spain. Hieronymites (the Order of St Jerome) are an order of hermit monks, and their monastery at Yuste could well have provided a cell for the emperor, but he required living quarters of a superior standard, and came with a substantial retinue that also needed to be accommodated. He therefore commissioned the construction of a miniature palace on the hill below the cloister. His bedroom adjoined the monastery church, from which it was separated by a glazed door. This arrangement meant that he could attend mass without having to get out of bed, which was a great convenience for a man with gout. Charles had an informed interest in gardens, and at Yuste planted his own with citrus fruit and fragrant herbs. In the middle of the garden terrace there was a well-stocked pond, and the retired emperor could fish from his study balcony to secure fresh tench for the royal table on fast days. Most hermits live austerely, but clearly Charles had no enthusiasm for an uncomfortable mode of eremetical living.

In the event, the emperor served as a hermit-monk for only two years. Shortly before his death in 1558 he asked his son, King Philip II of Spain, to construct an appropriate tomb. The result was the Escorial, which combines a royal palace with a Hieronymite monastery, and accommodates the royal tomb. Like his father, Philip wished to live as a hermit-monk, so the king's private rooms were less lavish than the public rooms in the complex. He also followed his father in arranging for his bedroom to be so close to the church that he could remain in bed during mass, and in planting a garden.

In 1599 Francisco Gómez de Sandoval y Rojas (fifth Marqués de Denia and fourth Conde de Lerma) became the Duque de Lerma, and soon began the process of transforming Lerma (a few miles south of Burgos) into a capital worthy of his new dignity. Working with the royal architect Francisco de Moro, he designed a ducal palace, together with gardens, parks, and the town that would support the estate. Around the central square he commissioned monasteries and a collegiate church, all of which were connected to the palace by corridors. Beginning in 1610, he commissioned seven hermitages for the gardens, all of which were completed within ten years; the palace is now a hotel (*parador*), and one of the hermitages, La Piedad, has survived.

The hermitages of Lerma constituted one of three precedents for the greatest of all garden hermitages, built in the garden of Buen

Retiro, the royal palace commissioned by King Philip IV on the eastern edge of Madrid, his new capital. The second precedent for Retiro was the Benedictine monastery of Montserrat (Catalonia), which the king visited in 1626. The mountain on which the monastery is situated had accommodated hermits for centuries, initially living in caves and later in purpose-built hermitages, each with a chapel, garden, orchard, and water cistern. At the time of the king's visit there were seven hermitages, of which two now survive (Santa Creu and Sant Dimas) and five are in ruins. The king decided to commission his own hermitages, beginning later in 1626 with the construction of thirteen hermitages (modelled on those at Montserrat) in the royal gardens at Aranjuez, south of Madrid. None now survives, as this stage of the garden has been overlaid by subsequent gardens, but these hermitages were the third precedent for Buen Retiro.

Buen Retiro was a vast project, and the king undertook it in stages. He began with the palace, and in 1634, when the first stage of construction was largely completed, he turned to the gardens. The acquisition of additional land enabled the king to commission an *allée* linking the Retiro to the garden of a nearby Dominican friary; the king regularly invited the friars to royal festivities in the garden. The presence of friars was not the only spiritual dimension of the garden. Indeed, its most distinctive feature was a set of seven hermitages. These were not the sort of basic accommodation appropriate to a community of hermits vowed to poverty, but rather architect-designed villas whose appearance echoed that of the palace. All seven were built of brick, with stone mouldings and slate roofs, and with the exception of San Pablo (St Paul), the first to be built, all had pointed towers. San Pablo was a distinctly Italianate building, especially in its ornate façade with recesses for statues, and indeed may have been designed by an Italian, Giovanni Battista Crescenzi. Its features included a capacious garden of which the centrepiece was a triple fountain of Narcissus. The other hermitages seem likely to have been designed by Spaniards. The largest, San Antonio de Padua, had a marble portal surmounted by a marble statue of the saint; the distinctive feature of this hermitage was its moat, which was linked to the large lake (still present in modified form) in the park. The most splendid, the hermitage of San Juan (St John the Baptist), was often occupied by the Conde-Duque de Olivares, royal favourite and prime minister.

It is difficult to judge the balance between the spiritual and secular uses of these hermitages. A modern sensibility is struck by the secular occasions for which they served as venues. Those dedicated to San Bruno and Santa María Magdalena, for example, were sometimes used for royal picnics or theatrical performances. What is less apparent to a modern sensibility is the ease with which some strands of Counter-Reformation spirituality could accommodate secular social occasions. The primary purpose of the hermitages was their representation of a type of pastoral devotion which was then in fashion. The juxtaposition of sacred and profane is perhaps most apparent in a commission given in 1638 to the sculptor Antonio de Herrera Barnuevo to carve (in wood) images of *Venus and Adonis* and a group of the *Three Magi* for the hermitage of San Jerónimo (St Jerome).

The spiritual significance of the hermitages of Buen Retiro was real, but so was the fact that they had become settings for courtly occasions. The element of fashion had begun to occlude the religious significance, but that transition would not be complete until the fashion reached England. The hermits were another matter. They may have been court hermits, but their spirituality remained uncompromised.

The last North European garden to have real hermits was established by Franz Anton Graf von Sporck (Czech: František Antonín Špork), who is best known for his founding of the first opera house and company in Bohemia. In the early decades of the eighteenth century Count von Sporck established five hermitages (dedicated to Saints Francis, Paul, Anthony, Bruna, and Giles) in the grounds of his estate near the spa town of Kuks (German Kuckus), in the 'New Forest' (Czech Nový Les, German Neuwald) in Bohemia (now the Czech Republic). Count von Sporck was a deeply religious Catholic, albeit of a liberal persuasion, and these were real hermits living in real forest hermitages. The hermitages, which are illustrated in a biography of Count von Sporck published in 1720, were modest wooden buildings in a contemporary vernacular idiom. Details of what happened to Count von Sporck's hermits are obscure, but it seems that in about 1720 three of his hermits were accused of heresy and dismissed after trial in an ecclesiastical court. They were replaced by a gallery of stone hermits that were part of the baroque extravaganza of sculpture carved out of rocky outcrops by Matyáš Bernard Braun, and many of these hermits can still be seen; indeed, they are the greatest monument of high baroque sculpture in central Europe. In due course Count von Sporck followed his hermits into the courtroom, because his dislike of Counter-Reformation zealotry led in 1729 to a falling out with the Jesuits of Žíreč. A church court confiscated his library (which contained books on the 'Index' of forbidden books), and it took Count von Sporck until 1734 (four years before his death) to clear his name.

In Italy garden hermits lasted longer. Villa Cetinale, near Siena, was the creation of Fabio Chigi (who became Pope Alexander VII in 1655), his nephew Cardinal Flavio Chigi, and Flavio's nephew Cardinal Anton Felice Chigi-Zondadari. The architect of the late seventeenth-century phase of construction was Carlo Fontana, who designed for Cardinal Anton Felice the garden staircase and the building known as the Romitorio, a five-storey hermitage (completed 1713–16) which has recently been restored. The Chigi installed hermits in the Romitorio, and hermits were to remain in residence until the nineteenth century. They may have been Europe's last religious garden hermits.

The secular court hermitage

In ordinary English usage the term 'hermitage' denotes the simple home of someone who from religious motives has withdrawn from society to live a solitary life. Less frequently, the term is used to denote a retreat built for a ruler wanting to withdraw from his official residence. The architectural original of the ruler's retreat is the small house constructed on an island at Hadrian's villa (AD 118–34), near Tivoli (east of Rome). The house is a villa in miniature, with vestibule, bedroom, dining-room, bathing suite, and courtyard, and it is surrounded by a moat. The most distinctive feature of the design, in which the Emperor seems to have had a hand, is that the rooms are defined by curves rather than straight lines. The building was topped with umbrella domes, which occasioned the caustic comment of one ancient architect (Apollodorus of Damascus) about Hadrian's enthusiasm for pumpkins.

With the fall of the Roman Empire, Hadrian's villa disappeared from public view, and for a millennium the site was used as a quarry, until the humanists and artists of the late fifteenth century began to visit it. A century later Pirro Ligorio, the papal architect, began to excavate the villa in what is now regarded as the first modern archaeological dig. In 1558 Ligorio began work on a small garden house for Pope Paul IV, designed as a retreat for the pontiff. The building draws on the tradition of the *villa suburbana* inaugurated by Pope Innocent VIII when he commissioned the Villa Belvedere on the high ground above the Vatican in 1484, but the debt to Hadrian's miniature villa is readily apparent: the purpose of the *villa suburbana* was recreation in a social setting, whereas Paul IV's villa, like Hadrian's, was designed to facilitate solitude. The elegant house (which now houses the Pontifical Academy of Sciences) stands in the gardens of the Vatican, but is nonetheless a secular building, in the sense that it was designed as a comfortable place for the pope to withdraw for a few hours rather than an austere home for a hermit. The villa complex has a free-standing loggia and an oval courtyard with fountains and a bench around the perimeter. The exterior decoration honours the life of Pius IV, in whose pontificate the building was completed, and after whom it is named (it is known as La Casina di Pio IV); the interior is sumptuously decorated with paintings and stuccowork.

Hadrian's villa and its tiny retreat proved to be among the most influential buildings in the history of architecture. Its centralized plan was mostly memorably recapitulated by Andrea Palladio in the Villa Rotonda, which is contemporary with the Casina di Pio IV. The idea of the small retreat close to the official residence became fashionable in Italian gardens, notably at the Villa Farnese in Caprarola (north-west of Rome), where in the 1560s a Casino del Piacere ('house of pleasure') designed by Jacopo Vignola was built in a sumptuous 'secret garden' (*giardino segreto*) 400 metres from the main house. In France, Louis XIV commissioned a royal château (1679–83) at Marly (west of Paris), where he erected the Pavillon du Roi, a square two-storey house with four identical façades. The design of this *maison de plaisance*, the setting for royal house parties, reached back through the *casini* of Renaissance Italy to Hadrian's villa. In the grounds there were twelve smaller pavilions that were meant to evoke the idea of the hermit's cell.

The buildings at Marly were imitated in Germany, where in 1715 Markgraf Georg Wilhelm von Brandenburg-Bayreuth (a Lutheran) commissioned the architect Johann David Räntz the elder to construct a small palace known as the Hermitage (German: Eremitage) just outside Bayreuth. The palace (1715–18; altered 1743–54) consisted of a four-winged main building (faced with an illusionistic imitation of a rock wall); the side wings accommodated twelve-room suites for the hermit and the lady hermit (*Einsiedlerdamen*). Buildings in the park included a grotto, a banqueting house, and several small hermitages intended to accommodate the Markgraf and his court when they pretended to be hermits, submitting themselves to a comfortable version of the simple life and the austere rules of an imaginary order of hermits. Although the aristocratic hermits slept in their huts, dinner was taken in the palace. A later Markgraf, Friedrich von Brandenburg-Bayreuth, commissioned a similar fantasy at Zwernitz Castle near Wonsees, where in 1744 he began to create the Sanspareil Felsengarten ('rock garden without equal'). In the course of the next four years he and the Markgräfin Wilhelmine created a series of gardens with small buildings (including a ruined theatre) and caves and rocks named after incidents in the life of Telemachus as described in Fénelon's pedagogical romance, *Les Aventures de Télémaque*; one of the caves contained a statue of a hermit reading a treatise by Paracelsus. The Sanspareil Hermitage (the Morgenländische Bau) designed by the Bayreuth court architect Joseph Saint-Pierre was a small palace (still extant) built to furnish comfortable accommodation for aristocratic hermits.

It is easy to see such projects as whimsical frivolity, and on one level the court hermitage was indeed play-acting, but there was also an idealistic dimension based on Rousseau. The court hermitage afforded an opportunity for those born into the nobility to illustrate their natural nobility by living solitary lives in simple buildings in natural settings.

Many grand buildings gesture towards the eremetical life through their names. In America the magnificent plantation home (near Nashville) of President Andrew Jackson is known as The Hermitage. It has a Greek Revival interior (lined with wallpaper made for it in Paris) and a fine Palladian façade. The name, which was bestowed by President Jackson, originally referred to the cluster of log buildings in which the Jackson family lived when he first acquired the property, but then became the name of the mansion to which Jackson retired after his second term as president.

The apogee of the court hermitage is the palace commissioned by Catherine the Great in St Petersburg. Its precedents include Peterhof (known from 1944 to 1974 as Petrodvorets), the summer palace of Peter the Great on the shore of the Gulf of Finland, 30 kilometres/20 miles from St Petersburg. Peterhof, which was inspired by Versailles, was constructed in the course of the eighteenth century to designs by a series of distinguished foreign architects. The garden hermitage, an elegant classical building with Corinthian pilasters, is a small palace by the sea, designed by Johann Friedrich Braunstein; work commenced in 1721 and was completed shortly after the emperor's death in 1725. The hermitage was designed for dining: a kitchen on the ground floor was surmounted by a dining-room (with seating for fourteen) on the upper floor. At first there was no staircase, so guests had to be hoisted up to the dining-room on a chairlift. The dining-table could be lowered to the kitchen below to be laden with food before rising again to the dining-room, so ensuring that the emperor and his guests could speak without being overheard. In 1797 the chairlift malfunctioned and left the tsar (Paul I) stranded in mid-air, whereupon a staircase was constructed.

Bartolomeo Francesco Rastrelli was the architect of the Tsaritsa Elizabeth (the daughter of Peter the Great), and his work for her included Yekaterinsky Palace (1749–56) at Tsarskoe Selo ('the tsar's village', now Pushkin). The garden has a hermitage by Rastrelli and a neo-Gothic hermitage kitchen, replete with turrets and pinnacles, designed by Vasily Ivanovich Neyelov, who had studied landscape gardening in England. Elizabeth described her private apartment in the Winter Palace in St Petersburg as her hermitage, so she had access to hermitages in all seasons.

Catherine the Great acceded to the throne in 1762, and one of her first architectural commissions was a 'hermitage' in St Petersburg. This was a small palace attached to the Winter Palace, and it was designed as a retreat from the affairs of state conducted in the adjoining palace. The language of Catherine's court was French, and Catherine named her retreat the Ermitage, which acknowledged her predecessors Peter the Great and Elizabeth and gestured towards the European fashion for the ideals of Rousseau. The original Petit Ermitage (1764–7) was extended during Catherine's reign by the buildings now known as the Old Hermitage and the New Hermitage, and it is this complex (together with some building in the 1840s) that is now known as the Hermitage. Catherine's enactment of the simple life as extolled by Rousseau took the form of informal dinner parties at which guests could choose where to sit. Instead of a footman standing behind each guest to serve the food, Catherine used a system of service without servants, or at least without visible servants: food arrived on a dumb waiter from the kitchen below. The same device was used by (and perhaps invented by) Thomas Jefferson at Monticello (the Palladian retreat depicted on the back of the American nickel), so enabling the president to entertain with only one servant in the dining-room. The idea of a single servant in the dining-room may not seem like modest living to most twenty-first-century people, but my battered copy of the fifth edition of the *Concise Oxford Dictionary* (1963) defines the 'simple life' as 'the practice of doing without servants and luxuries'. Catherine owned serfs and Jefferson owned slaves, but in their hermitages they achieved the ideal of the simple life.

The most elaborate architectural manifestation of the courtly ideal of the simple life is the *hameau* (hamlet) of Queen Marie-Antoinette at Versailles, a *ferme ornée* (ornamented farm) built in the grounds of the Petit Trianon, which King Louis XVI had given to her as a private retreat in 1774. This group of 'peasant' buildings (1783–5), arranged around a small artificial lake, was designed by Richard Mique, the Queen's architect. The architectural ensemble includes the Queen's house, a watermill, a dairy, a fishery, and several peasant

FIGURE 1.1 The *hameau* of Queen Marie-Antoinette at Versailles.

houses. The *hameau* enabled the queen, her ladies, and her children to act out Rousseau's ideals of sensibility, innocence, and nature in a secure setting unaffected by any need to pay the bills or fend off the indigent. We shall return to those ideals in the next chapter, but in the interim must attend to developments in England.

Elizabethan garden buildings

The gatehouses of medieval England gradually evolved into the park gate lodges of the eighteenth and nineteenth centuries. In the intervening period, particularly in the late sixteenth and early seventeenth centuries, the garden pavilion became a popular form, and it could be located either at the gate or within the garden. What distinguishes the pavilion from its predecessors and successors is its occupants: gatehouses and park gate lodges were occupied by estate servants, whereas pavilions were designed for the use of the proprietors of the main house as well as (or instead of) estate servants. Pavilions close to the house were known as 'banquet' houses, and were often used for dining: small pavilions were used in the summer for the consumption of dessert while the main tables were being cleared, and large pavilions, equipped with fireplaces, could be used throughout the year for entire meals. The best-known of these Elizabethan pavilions, by virtue of its arcane symbolism, its architectural design, and its proximity to the railway line north from London, is the triangular lodge built by Sir Thomas Tresham at Rushton (Northamptonshire) in the 1590s. In the estate accounts the building is always called 'the warrener's lodge', which indicates that it was used by the estate servant responsible for rabbits, but the lavish decoration of the top floor of the interior clearly indicates that room was intended for the social use of the Tresham family.

Lodges were not hermitages, but the various architectural forms of seventeenth-century garden buildings anticipate the classical, Gothic, and *cottage ornée* styles of eighteenth-century garden hermitages.

Earlier British hermits

The fourth precedent for the secular English hermit is the British hermit in earlier centuries. There have been hermits and hermitages in Britain and Ireland since Christianity was established in the Atlantic archipelago, but the precise date at which a Christian church was established is not known. By 314 the British church was sufficiently well organized to send two bishops to the Council of Arles. The evidence of hermits before that date is distinctly thin, but in 304 hermits called Julius and Aaron are said in medieval sources to have been martyred at Carleon (south Wales) in the persecution initiated by the emperor Diocletian. This may not be true (there is doubt about whether Diocletian's persecution was ever implemented in Britain), but what is certain that, in the course of the next millennium, hundreds of hermitages were established in Britain. A century ago Rotha Mary Clay listed in her *Hermits and Anchorites of England* some 750 cells in England, together with the names of more than 650 hermits and anchorites. The largest organized group of hermits was the Carthusian Order, which had ten houses (known as Charterhouses) in England; a Carthusian hermit's cell in Mount Grace Priory (now owned by English Heritage) in Yorkshire has recently been restored.

The tradition of religious hermits was disrupted by the dissolution of the monasteries (1536–9) and the suppression of the chantries (1546), but was restored when the Carthusians returned to England in 1873, and there is now a Charterhouse in West Sussex with 34 hermitages. In the intervening centuries, hermits and hermitages were all secular. The first documented secular hermitage in the British Isles was built in 1621 by the mining entrepreneur and former mintmaster Thomas Bushell, who at several points in his life lived as a secular hermit. Bushell had been a member of Francis Bacon's staff, and when Bacon was deposed as chancellor in 1621, his staff were implicated in accusations of corruption. In a gesture of contrition, Bushell retired to a cabin on the Calf of Man, where he lived as a self-proclaimed hermit for three years.

> in obedience to my dead lord's [Bacon's] philosophical advice, I resolved to make a perfect experiment upon myself, for the obtaining of a long and healthy life, most necessary for such a repentance as my

> former debauchedness required, by a parsimonious diet of herbs, oil,
> mustard, and honey, with water sufficient ... as was conceived by that
> lord, which I most strictly observed as if obliged by a religious vow.

The final phrase marks Bushell's standing as a transitional figure
between the religious hermits of pre-Reformation Britain and the
secular garden hermits of the Georgian period.

After leaving the Calf of Man, Bushell returned to London and
married an heiress, whose money he used to buy a small estate at
Enstone, near Chipping Norton, in Oxfordshire. There he built a
grotto around a spring and a distinctive rock ('with pendants like ici-
cles', says John Aubrey). The complex included a two-room hermitage in a Gothic idiom; one room was a bedroom and the other a
hermit's cell, hung with black cloths 'representing a melancholy
retired life like a hermit's'. The antiquary Abraham Pryme recorded
in his memoir of Bushell that when he had turned his hermitage into
'a kind of a paradise', he resolved 'to take up his habitation therein all
the days of his life, like as the famous Guy, Earl of Warwick, did in his
cliff yet to be seen near Warwick' (on which see p. 28–9). Bushell's
hermitage and the waterworks in his grotto soon began to attract
aristocratic visitors, and in 1634 Bushell's guests included King
Charles I. Lieutenant Hammond, who visited in 1635, noted this
royal visit and went on to praise the 'admirable' building, but frowned
on 'the hermit's diet drink, the clear rock water', and so departed for
nearby Tew, which had taverns in which he and his colleagues could
find 'a cup of better liquor'. The following year the king returned
with Queen Henrietta Maria, and on this occasion Bushell prepared
an entertainment which began with 'the hermit's speech ascending
out of the ground as the King entered the rock'. This entertainment
survives, because Bushell published the 'several speeches and songs'.

The various accounts of visitors to the site make it clear that Bushell's hermitage garden was modelled on the secret gardens of Renaissance Italy; even the water games (*giochi d'acqua*) of these gardens were replicated at Enstone.

Enstone was confiscated in 1643, and the hermitage was subsequently turned into a banqueting room by Edward Lee, first earl of Lichfield. Bushell decamped to Lundy, where he lived as an island hermit (and as governor) for several years. Finally, Bushell went into hiding in a house in Lambeth (which was then isolated marshland), where 'in the garret', as Aubrey explains, 'there is a long gallery which [Bushell] hung all with black, and had some death's heads and bones painted'. This was Bushell's fourth hermitage; its setting within a house makes it a precedent for Sir John Soane's hermitage in Lincoln's Inn Fields.

The Bushell model of a hermit who retreated from the world after a personal crisis had a long afterlife in figures such as John Bigg, who was a clerk of the regicide Symon Mayne. When Mayne died in prison in 1661, Bigg retired from the world into a cave in Mayne's estate, Dinton Hall (Buckinghamshire), and there lived for 36 years. His habit of patching his clothes and shoes by adding fresh pieces of cloth and leather over holes created patchwork clothes and shoes many layers thick, as John Aubrey noted. One of Bigg's shoes is now in the Ashmolean, and the other is still at Dinton Hall. Although Bigg was posthumously regarded as picturesque, as can be seen from the portrait on the sign of the pub called the Dinton Hermit in nearby Ford, he and his equally wretched successors were not ornamental, and so are a byway in terms of the development of the ornamental hermit.

2

The Idea of the Hermit

The phenomenon of the ornamental hermit is not easily understood. At its core lies a notion of contemplative solitude and
pleasurable melancholy, but it was also a fashion. I propose to eluci-
date the strands of Georgian culture that produced the garden hermit by examining five contexts: the horticultural, the antiquarian,
the philosophical, the literary, and the architectural.

The horticultural context

The evolution of garden design in English gardens is not a tidy story
of new designs replacing their predecessors, for at least three reasons.
First, new fashions and traditional styles often existed alongside each
other, and, as in all stylistic innovations, it was never clear which new
fashions would survive as long-term trends. Second, some strands of
period design lived on or were revived in subsequent periods: the 'wildernesses' introduced in the Elizabethan period, for example, reap-
peared in some eighteenth-century gardens. Indeed, as late as 1813,
when Jane Austen published *Pride and Prejudice*, Lady Catherine de

Bourgh could refer to 'a prettyish kind of a little wilderness' at Long-bourne (and Mrs Bennet could suggest that Elizabeth show Lady Catherine the hermitage). Third, there is a complex relationship with garden design on the Continent, in that England sometimes followed and sometimes led European fashions, but inevitably both designs and planting had to be adapted to varying climates and soils.

At the beginning of the eighteenth century, a range of influences was apparent in English gardens. Long-established Italian models persisted, but there were also new influences. Royalists who had returned from France with King Charles II in 1660 had introduced elements of French design, such as the magnificent canals at Hampton Court, Chatsworth, and Boughton House. Similarly, the accession of a Dutch monarch (William III) to the English throne in 1688 had occasioned a revival of Dutch models, with relatively small gardens characterized by features such as flower displays and evergreens in topiary form. Some designers worked within the context of these influences, aspiring to the grandeur of the French tradition and the careful attention to detail of the Dutch tradition, but others rebelled. The focal point of rebellion was a conviction that Continental gardens were products of artifice, and so too far removed from the emerging notion of the natural. In earlier centuries nature and the natural were deemed to be in need of the civilizing influences of order, but in this period the perception began to shift to the view (still in fashion in the twenty-first century) that nature is authentic and beneficent, and that the constructed environment is an undesirable artifice.

In gardening, the clarion call for 'natural' gardens came from Anthony Ashley Cooper, the Earl of Shaftesbury. One of those who responded to Shaftesbury's challenge was Alexander Pope, who decried fashions such as topiary and attempted to create a 'natural' garden at Twickenham, which was then a village on the Thames to the south-west of London. The conception that lay behind his five-acre garden was that of truth to the *genius loci*, the spirit of the place. In practice this meant enhancing natural characteristics and ensuring that buildings were sympathetic to this spirit. One of the features of Pope's innovative garden was a grotto (completed in 1725) incorporated into a tunnel that led from the riverside to the rear garden, underneath the villa and an intervening road. The villa and garden have gone, but the grotto survives, and is administered by a preservation trust.

The tunnel was a practicality, but Pope's grotto was invested with meaning. He thought of it as a place of withdrawal and peacefulness, and used it in much the same way that later landowners would use their hermitages: for contemplation and for entertaining friends. On occasion he styled himself 'the hermit of Twickenham'. He asked Judith Cowper (later Madan) if she would like him to 'describe my solitude and grotto to you', and in a poem composed for Lady Mary Wortley Montagu he listed the 'falling rills' of the grotto as one of the features of his garden that formed 'soft recesses for th'uneasy mind | To sigh unheard in'. These were sentiments that were soon to become associated with hermitages rather than grottoes, though there was always an element of overlap. Pope told Edward Blount that the grotto was 'in the natural taste', and Pope's notion of natural garden design was to prove immensely influential. His influence was often direct, because Pope often advised landowners on garden design; in Ireland his influence was indirect, in that his views were mediated through his friendship with Jonathan Swift and the Delanys.

The ideal of a 'natural' garden emerged at about the same time as the wish to create gardens that were distinctively English, and English themes became a feature of gardens such as Kew and Stowe, both of which incorporated displays of English worthies. The real Englishness of these gardens, however, lay in a determination to integrate pastoral, agrarian, and wooded landscapes into the garden, and to preserve or re-create ancient and medieval ruins in the garden. The first of these aims was achieved by the introduction of the ha-ha, a walled ditch (derived from the French *claire voie*) that kept grazing animals away from the house while allowing landscapes uninterrupted by fences or walls to be viewed from the house and garden. The second aim was achieved by retaining ruins (for example, those of Fountains Abbey at Studley Royal, or the ancient ruins at Stonor Park) or constructing classical temples or, at a later stage, Gothic ruins. Agricultural buildings deemed inappropriate to the landscape were refashioned or replaced by buildings in the *ferme ornée* tradition in estates such as Lord Bathurst's at Riskins (now Richings) Park, near Iver (Buckinghamshire) and Mrs Delany's at Delville, near Dublin. The great houses on estates designed in this new idiom tended to be Palladian, so the rustic hermitage that would soon appear in these gardens stood in marked contrast to the grandest of architectural styles.

The innovator of this new style was Charles Bridgeman, whose gardens included Stowe. His successor at Stowe and in the great tradition of English landscape gardeners was William Kent, who also designed Stourhead. The third landscape architect in this tradition was Lancelot 'Capability' Brown, who, early in his career, worked with Kent at Stowe and went on to become the most important landscape architect in England for two generations. Brown shifted the balance between buildings and landscape in favour of the latter, and created many magnificent landscapes of idealized nature.

Brown's Edenic creations represented the dominant fashion in gardening, but his naturalistic style coexisted with an alternative type of garden which became the habitat of the hermit. This was the associative garden, the garden of feeling, which began with Pope's garden at Twickenham and then became the guiding principle of gardens such as Painshill, Stourhead and the neighbouring estates of The Leasowes, Hagley and Enville. Later in the eighteenth century, another type of garden that was to become the habitat of hermits was the picturesque garden, which was particularly suited to the rugged landscapes of Scotland.

Until the eighteenth century, the design of English gardens was largely an adaptation of European styles, but with the English landscape garden of the eighteenth century the influence began to flow the other way, and a fashion for gardens in the English style swept through the Continent. It is this influence that accounts for hermitages and the occasional hermit in Continental gardens (see Appendix 2).

The antiquarian context

The phenomenon of the garden hermit is typically represented as emerging suddenly in the mid-eighteenth century and disappearing at the beginning of the nineteenth century. On closer investigation, however, it becomes clear that the idea of the hermit had an earlier manifestation in the figure of the druid and, as will become apparent in Chapter 6, a cultural afterlife in the twentieth century, ultimately as the keeper of the mathematical secret of the universe.

The druids were known in classical antiquity through the writings of Posidonius, a Greek traveller of the second century BC. His account of druidic priestly practices in Britain and Gaul did not survive, but before it was lost to history it had become the principal source of the later accounts by Strabo, Diodorus Siculus, and Tacitus, all of whom emphasized the grisly details of mass human sacrifice in druid ritual. The church fathers of the Alexandrian tradition, who were profoundly influenced by classical Platonism and Pythagoreanism, took a more benign view of druids, and fathers such as Clement of Alexandria, Origen, and (at a later date) St Cyril presented druids as keepers of the Pythagorean flame and students of the natural world. Neo-Pythagoreanism was for these purposes a religion based on mathematical principles and a commitment to a life of principled simplicity. When these texts were read in late sixteenth-century England the druids emerged as the bards of ancient Britain, and it was the late Alexandrian tradition (rather than the hostile classical tradition) that formed the basis of the seventeenth-century construction of the British druid.

The view of John Milton was typical. In 'Lycidas' he described the Welsh island of Bardsey as 'where your old bards, the famous druids, lie'. In *Areopagitica*, Milton dismissed the notion that classical philosophy had its origins in ancient Greece and Persia on the grounds that all good things begin in Britain, and that 'even the school of Pythagoras and the Persian wisdom took beginning from the old philosophy of this island'. That 'old philosophy' was the wisdom of the druids, who were thought to have transmitted their mathematics and religion (especially metempsychosis) to the Greeks and their command of magic to the Persian Zoroastrians. The idea that ancient Greek philosophy originated in Britain was part of a larger contention that all good things begin there. That meant, for example, that the Reformation could not have been initiated by Luther, because he had the misfortune to be a foreigner, but was rather the accomplishment of Wyclif. The reason, as Milton explains, is that God reveals himself 'first to his Englishmen'. Quite so.

The enduring popular image of the druid as a bearded and robed ancient British seer has its origins in the antiquarian William Camden's *Britannia* (1586), which was translated from Latin into English in 1610. This publication in turn informed the image of the druid as a primeval philosopher and patriot embodied in works such as Michael Drayton's massive poem *Polyolbion* (1612) and John Fletcher's play *Bonduca* (performed 1613–14, published 1647). When visual representations of druids began to appear, their costumes seem to have been influenced by the Sadeler prints of hermits that were to inform the architecture of the ornamental hermitage (see Figure 4.4, p. 109). The link between the druids and the ruins of Stonehenge and Avebury (then known as Abury) was first made by the antiquarian John Aubrey, whose *Monumenta Britannica* (not published till 1980) was in 1717 read in manuscript by the physician and antiquarian William Stukeley, who later published treatises on *Stonehenge, a Temple Restor'd to the British Druids* (1740) and *Abury, a Temple of the British Druids* (London, 1743).

William Stukeley is the central character in the story of the emergence of the hermitage in the garden. In the early 1720s he was living in London, where he became a Fellow of the Royal Society, a Fellow of the Royal College of Physicians, a Grand Master of the Masons, and a founding member of the Society of Antiquaries. His life changed in 1726, when, as he recorded in his commonplace book, 'an irresistible impulse seized my mind to leave the town', and he accordingly left London to settle in Grantham (Lincolnshire) as a country doctor. In 1728 he married a local woman, in 1729 he was ordained in the Church of England, and in 1730 he moved to Stamford (Lincolnshire), where he was to serve as vicar of All Saints for eighteen years. His ecclesiastical duties were not taxing, and Stukeley was able to devote time to gardening and antiquarianism. It was during these years that he wrote his books on Stonehenge and Avebury. During this period he lived in three houses (one in Grantham and two on Barn Hill in Stamford) and landscaped all three gardens.

In a letter of 15 July 1727 Stukeley described to his fellow physician Richard Mead (15 July 1727) a wall that he was building in his Grantham garden, which had been designed to resemble a druidic grove:

> it is made after the manner of the front of a Greek temple; within, upon the wall which is plastered, I have painted Sir Isaac Newton's profile, which I had taken very exactly.... next, my herb garden; it represents the ruins of some old religious house, and there is made in the wall a cell or grotto, which I call the hermitage, like those I have frequently seen in travels.

The image of Newton anticipates the bust of Newton that Queen Caroline was to install in her hermitage several years later. The cave that most clearly caught the eye of Stukeley in his travels was Guy's Cliffe, near Warwick. This was the same cave adduced by Abraham Pryme in describing Bushell's hermitage. Stukeley records in his *Itinerarium Curiosum* that

> we were shown the sword and other gigantic relics of Guy the famous earl of Warwick. A mile out of town, on the side of a hill, is a pretty retired cell, called Guy-cliffe. We saw the rough cave where they say Guy died a hermit.

Guy of Warwick was the eponym of the influential thirteenth-century Anglo-Norman romance *Gui de Warewic*. After a career slaying infidels, giants, and dragons, Guy returned to Warwick disguised as a hermit. His disguise was so effective that even his wife Felice, who fed him in his cave, failed to recognize him until, as he lay dying, he sent her the gold ring that she had given to him. Chroniclers and antiquarians assumed the adventures of Guy to be rooted in historical fact: relics eventually began to emerge at Warwick Castle (where his sword can still be seen), and the Beauchamp earls traced their family line to Guy. The combination of a saintly life, exotic adventures, bloody but righteous violence, and a love story, gave the legend wide appeal, in addition to which its celebration of Athelstan's resistance to the Danes made it a nationalist poem that contributed very considerably to the construction of an English national identity. The legend of Guy, like that of the bardic druids, became annexed to an imagined English past. His cave is on property now owned by the Freemasons and administered by the Friends of Guy's Cliffe House, but is not open to the public.

On moving to Stamford in 1730 Stukeley lived at the All Saints vicarage (now 16 Barn Hill) for ten years and then moved to a larger house (now 9 Barn Hill). It was in the garden of this larger house that he constructed a druidic stone circle with a hermitage at the back, and filled the garden with architectural salvage in a Gothic style. Adornments included sculpture, stained glass, and the remains of the Stamford Eleanor Cross (now in the Stamford Museum), which he excavated in December 1745. It is this garden that Stukeley sketched in 1738, and the drawing survives in the Bodleian Library.

Antiquarian druidism overlapped very considerably with the idea of the hermit. Fredrik Magnus Piper, the artist who drew the

FIGURE 2.1 William Stukeley, pen-and-ink drawing of the hermitage, Stamford, Lincolnshire, 1738.

hermitage at Stourhead, headed his drawing (in Swedish) 'Plan and Profile of the Hermitage called the Druid's Cell' (see Plate 1). On occasion hermits were distinguished from druids (Hawkstone had both), but for the most part the two were conflated. Sometimes druidic stone circles were placed near hermitages, as Joseph Pocklington did at Derwentwater, and, in the late twentieth century, at Glin Castle, where the Knight of Glin constructed a druid's circle in front of an eighteenth-century hermitage. Druidism was deemed to be monotheistic, and William Stukeley thought that there was some evidence that the druids had anticipated the Christian doctrine of the trinity. The hermitages of Georgian Britain were secular, inasmuch as the picturesque was a secular movement, but they were often capped with crosses, so asserting that ornamental druids and hermits were not inconsistent with Christianity.

The philosophical context

The secularizing of the hermit required a new ideology, and that was to be supplied by the eighteenth-century *philosophe* Jean-Jacques Rousseau, a seminal advocate of the notion of the uncorrupted natural world, and a man who valued wilderness. Rousseau was a native of Geneva, and although Geneva was not admitted to the Swiss Confederation until 1815, he is rightly claimed as Switzerland's greatest writer. Indeed, he was arguably the most influential author ever to write in French. With respect to landscape gardening, he deplored the contemporary taste for gardens laid out in geometrical patterns and planted with cultivars, and instead championed untamed nature and praised wild flowers, natural shapes, virgin forests, and even the high mountains which his contemporaries so disliked (they preferred fertile plains that had been cultivated). This advocacy of the natural world transformed European perceptions of wilderness, which we now value largely because of Rousseau. He was also a champion of solitude, and the ideal of being alone and slightly melancholy proved enormously influential. Indeed, the ornamental hermits who will be discussed in the next chapter are embodiments of Rousseau's ideal.

It was Rousseau's *Julie, ou la nouvelle Héloïse* (1761) that set the agenda for the English landscape garden from the 1760s onwards. This was an epistolary novel consisting, as the original title explained, of *Lettres de deux amans habitans d'une petite ville au pied des Alpes* ('Letters from two lovers living in a small town at the foot of the Alps'). At one point in the novel (Part 4, Letter 11) the heroine, Julie, entertains her former lover in the garden that she has created. This Elysée, as the garden is called, formed the basis of one section of the picturesque garden of Ermenonville (near Senlis, north of Paris) laid out by Rousseau's friend Louis-René, marquis of Girardin. Ermenonville is a *jardin anglais*, largely based on The Leasowes. Ermenonville's debts to *La nouvelle Héloïse* include the Rustic Temple, the Monument to Old Loves, the Tower of Clarence, and the grove known as the Bocage. There was also an ornamental hermitage, again in imitation of The Leasowes. In 1778 Rousseau accepted an invitation to live at Ermenonville, where he was accommodated in a rubble-built thatched cabin with a view of the lake. He died at Ermenonville six weeks later; it is to be hoped that his death was not occasioned by the Spartan nature of his cabin.

The garden was visited and admired by many English landowners, and exercised a very considerable influence on English landscape garden design. The best example is perhaps Nuneham Courtenay, the Oxfordshire home of the Rousseauist George Simon Harcourt (second earl of Harcourt), where William Mason created a garden modelled on Julie's Elysée, with a quotation from *La nouvelle Héloïse* at the entrance and a statue of the Man of Nature with an inscription:

> Say is the heart to virtue warm?
> Can genius animate the feeling breast?
> Approach, behold this venerable form
> Tis ROUSSEAU, let thy bosom speak the rest!

In 1789 Lady Harcourt organized a feast at Nuneham Courtenay in imitation of the *fête de la vertu* mounted by Julie on the lawn of her garden. Lady Harcourt presented the most virtuous villagers (by the measures of cleanliness and diligence) with red letter 'M's (M for Merit). She also displayed two moralizing pictures on the lawn, one showing a well-scrubbed model village family (which the villagers wreathed with roses) and the other an unwashed reprobate family (which the villagers wreathed with nettles). An account of the

Nuneham feast published in the *Annual Register* in August 1789 seems to be the source of 'Henry and Eliza', an early Jane Austen story which satirizes the feast. Similarly, the English translation of *La nouvelle Héloïse* (*Eloisa: Or, a series of original letters collected and published by J. J. Rousseau*) published in four volumes in 1761 became immensely influential, in part because of the congruence with the ideal of sensibility which had emerged in eighteenth-century Britain. This notion, which is embodied in works such as Henry Mackenzie's sentimental novel *The Man of Feeling* (1771), presented strong emotional responsiveness as a virtue that endowed the sensitive person with an awareness of beauty and truth. Sensibility was in this respect a good thing, but it brought with it a melancholic disposition. This state of mind was deemed to be a sign of emotional insight and depth. The idea of sensibility was mocked by many, but not by those for whom it was an appropriate state of mind for the hermit and the visitor to the hermitage.

It is difficult to judge the spirit in which hermitages were built and hermits employed, but one architect, Sir John Soane, was particularly articulate about the matter. Soane is rightly associated with his principal achievement: the Bank of England. He is therefore naturally assumed to be a classical architect. From the outset, however, the classical purity of the Bank was called into question: an anonymous poet excoriated 'pilasters scored like loin of pork...scrolls fixed below and pedestals above...[and] defiance hurled at Greece and Rome'. The criticism may be unjust for an architect who asserted that 'art cannot go beyond the Corinthian order', but it does hint at another strand in Soane's complex architectural vision.

The clearest articulation of this unclassical strand lies in an early commission. In 1781 Philip Yorke (later third earl of Hardwicke), who had met Soane in Italy when both were on the Grand Tour, commissioned Soane to design buildings for Hamels, his Hertfordshire estate. These buildings included a rustic dairy (constructed 1783), for which drawings survive in the Sir John Soane Museum and the Victoria and Albert Museum. These drawings, which were brought forward from an earlier commission by Elizabeth, Lady Craven, were sometimes annotated by Soane. On one of these drawings Soane wrote:

> The pillars are proposed to be of the Trunks of Elm Trees with the bark on, and Honey suckle & Woodbine planted at their feet, forming festoons &c. The Roof to be thatched & the ends of the Rafters to appear. Plans of two designs for a Dairy in the primitive manner of building.

The final phrase hints at Soane's debt to the primitive hut extolled by Marc-Antoine Laugier in *Essai sur l'architecture* (1753), which Soane had read with great diligence. His description of the interior reveals that by 'primitive' Soane did not mean cheap (the dairy cost £550 12s. 3½d.) or austere:

> The ceiling of the loggia is arched; the dairy also has a vaulted ceiling, enriched with large sunk panels, filled with roses, and other ornaments in stucco; the tables for the milk are of marble ... the walls are varnished and decorated, and the windows are of stained-glass in lead-work.

The designs for the dairy also reflect Soane's reverence for Rousseau and Goethe; indeed, he presented a copy of Goethe's *The Sorrows of Young Werther* to Lady Elizabeth (Mr Yorke's wife). It is this sensibility that informs the eremetical part of Sir John Soane's house in Lincoln's Inn Fields, now one of London's most delightful house museums.

Soane was eager to make the wonders of his London house available to possible clients and to his students at the Royal Academy, and in 1830 he issued the first edition of the *Description of the house and museum on the north side of Lincoln's Inn Fields: the residence of John Soane, Architect*, which was considerably expanded for the second edition of 1835. For a student of hermits and hermitages, the most compelling part of the house is in the basement, where in 1824 Soane built a monastic suite consisting of a parlour (which Soane called the 'Parloir of Padre Giovanni'), the Monk's Cell (or Oratory), and the Monk's Yard. The word 'parloir' (an archaic spelling of 'parlour') is used in the sense of a room in a monastery set aside for conversation with visitors. Soane placed in the parlour a selection of objects designed, as he explained, 'to impress the spectator with reverence for the monk'; one of these objects is an eighteenth-century carved wooden figure of a monk, which Soane declared to be a portrait of Padre Giovanni. The tables in the parlour, both designed by William Kent, are painted black to accentuate the melancholy mood of the room. The monk's cell contains a fifteenth-century Flemish wooden crucifixion. Through the window the visitor can see the Monk's Yard, which was wonderfully restored in 2006. Soane created the impression of monastic ruins in a tiny urban space by using architectural salvage from the palace of Westminster Hall and St Stephen's Chapel in Westminster, parts of which were rebuilt when Soane was working on government buildings as an architect to the Office of Works. The cloister of the Monk's Yard, for example, consists of two window openings from the medieval House of Lords, which was demolished in 1822 to make way for Soane's Royal Gallery. The yard also accommodates the tomb of Padre Giovanni.

Soane's description of the Monk's Yard, in which he invited visitors to wander, is an excellent account of the spirit in which the monastic complex was constructed:

> The ruins of a monastery arrest the attention.... The rich canopy and other decorations of this venerable spot are objects which cannot fail to produce the most powerful sensations in the minds of the admirers of the piety of our forefathers.... The tomb of the monk adds to the gloomy scenery of this hallowed place.... The pavement, composed of the tops and bottoms of broken bottles and pebbles found amongst the gravel dug out for the foundation of the monastery, and disposed in symmetry of design, furnishes an admirable lesson of simplicity and economy, and shows the unremitting assiduity of the pious monk. The stone structure at the head of the monk's grave contains the remains of Fanny, the faithful companion, the delight, the solace of his leisure hours. Alas, poor Fanny.

The final phrase, a humorous echo of Hamlet's 'Alas, poor Yorick', commemorates Padre Giovanni's dog, but the dog buried there, a Manchester Terrier called Fanny, belonged to Mrs (later Lady) Soane. The description therefore combines frivolity with a purposeful intention of provoking 'powerful sensations' on those wandering in the yard. As the yard is only a few square yards, wandering is of necessity limited, so the sombre tone of the description is subverted by an undercurrent of self-deprecating humour. On the other hand, Soane offers a shrewd rationale for the patterned pebble floors of so many ornamental hermitages.

Soane goes on to discuss Padre Giovanni, whose name is the Italian version of 'John' and whose title is the Italian title of a priest:

> It may, perhaps, be asked, before leaving this part of the museum, at what period the monk existed whose masonry is here preserved, and whether he is to be identified with any of those whose deeds have enshrined their names. The answer to these questions is furnished by Horace: *dulce est desipere in loco.*

The phrase from Horace has become a proverb, most memorably articulated by Roald Dahl's Willy Wonka: 'A little nonsense now and then is relished by the wisest men'. Padre Giovanni is on the one hand 'a little nonsense', but one does not have to be a Freudian (and I am not) to see that on another level he embodies the pronounced melancholic strain in the character of John Soane, who was often morose. Reflecting darkly on the (imagined) conspiracies directed against him, Soane also identified himself with Rousseau. The public face of Soane was that of a great architect whose prestigious interiors included the dining-rooms of Nos. 10 and 11 Downing Street (both 1825), but within his home (which was a more public space than the dining-rooms of Downing Street) he assumed a different persona, a dark and brooding figure whose temperament was represented in Padre Giovanni.

The literary context

The hermit has been a constant character in English literature since the Anglo-Saxon period, when the lives of three hermits were celebrated. Cuthbert, the seventh-century bishop of Lindisfarne who lived as a hermit on the islands now known as Hobthrush (or St Cuthbert's Isle) and Inner Farne, became a central figure in Bede's imaginative historical narratives and of a poem in Latin hexameters. Guthlac, the eighth-century hermit of Crowland (Lincolnshire), became the subject of a poem that endows the hermit with heroic qualities. Neot, the ninth-century hermit of what is now St Neot (near Bodmin Moor), was later honoured by four biographies (three Latin and one Old English), one of which incorporated stories borrowed from legends of Irish saints. In the Middle English period, when the figure of the hermit regularly appears in legends of saints and devotional literature, the hermit became a source of wisdom to his visitors. The *Alphabet of Tales*, a popular fifteenth-century English translation of the *Alphabetum narrationum* (now attributed to Arnold of Liège), contains many stories of exemplary incidents in the lives of hermits. The hermit is also a standard character in the chivalric romances of the later Middle Ages.

At the Reformation real hermits disappeared, crushed by the dissolution of the monasteries (1536) and the suppression of the chantries (1547). Hermits became creatures of the imagination who appeared on stages and in print. When Queen Elizabeth visited Woodstock in 1575, the entertainments mounted by Sir Henry Lee included George Gascoyne's *Tale of Hemetes the Hermit*; Lee later wrote several poems in honour of the Queen, cast in the persona of a hermit. Similarly, when the Queen visited Theobalds in 1591, there was a 'Hermit's speech' written by George Peele and spoken by Robert Cecil (later earl of Salisbury) in which the 'hermit of Theobalds' apologizes for the absence of Lord Burghley (William Cecil, Robert's father), who was said to have withdrawn to the hermitage to mourn the death of his mother, his wife, and his daughter. When the Queen returned three years later, Sir Robert Cecil (who had been knighted on the occasion of the previous visit) composed a 'Hermit's Oration' in her honour.

At about the same time, the hermit was starting to appear as a moralizing figure in prose romances, such as John Lyly's *Euphues*, Robert Greene's *Arbasto*, and Emanuel Ford's *Parismus*, in all of which the hermit functions as a sage. There are also hermits in the poetry of the period, notably in Richard Lovelace's 'To Althea, from Prison', which in its final stanza declares that

> Stone walls do not a prison make,
> Nor Iron bars a cage;
> Minds innocent and quiet take
> That for an hermitage.

The association of the hermit with quietness of mind is extended by some poets to melancholy. At the conclusion of the anonymous 'Farewell to the vanities of the world' (possibly the work of Sir Walter Ralegh), for example, the poet withdrawing from the world declares:

> Then here I'll sit, and sigh my hot love's folly,
> And learn t' affect an holy melancholy.

It is a secular version of this sentiment that feeds into the thinking about garden hermits in the eighteenth century.

Finally, there is one sixteenth-century poet who creates a villainous hermit. In the opening canto of Spenser's *Faerie Queene*, Red Cross Knight is taken home by a stranger:

> A little lowly hermitage it was,
> Down in a dale, hard by a forest's side,
> Far from resort of people, that did pass
> In travel to and fro: a little wyde [i.e. apart]
> There was an holy chapel edified,
> Wherein the hermit duly wont to say
> His holy things each morn and eventide.

The hermit turns out to be the wicked Archimago. Although most eighteenth-century hermits were to be benign, there remained a niche in the horticultural imagination for the wicked hermit, and 'Archimago's Cell' featured among the designs of William Kent.

Of all the seventeenth-century poets, it is Milton that lies most heavily on the literature of the eighteenth century; mercifully, that hand rests more lightly on the landscape gardens of the period. The lines that appear most often on hermitages (such as Selborne, Hagley, and Lilliput Castle) are taken from Milton's 'Il Penseroso', the founding text of the eighteenth-century cult of melancholy.

> And may at last my weary age
> Find out the peaceful hermitage,
> The hairy gown and mossy cell,
> Where I may sit and rightly spell,
> Of every Star that Heav'n doth shew,
> And every Herb that sips the dew;
> Till old experience do attain
> To something like prophetic strain.
> These pleasures Melancholy give,
> And I with thee will choose to live.

Milton was at this stage a high church Anglican rather than the radical puritan he was later to become, but there were no hermits in the English church. Milton's only encounter with a real hermit came later, when he travelled from Rome to Naples in the company of a hermit. In this poem he is invoking a hermit of the imagination, a figure who embodies visionary melancholia.

The idea of pleasurable melancholy seems odd to a modern reader, because we tend to think of 'melancholy' as an old-fashioned word for depression, but in the eighteenth century it was heartily embraced. At the end of the century, in Jane Austen's *Northanger Abbey* (written *c.*1799) Catherine Morland approaches 'a thick grove of old Scotch firs'; she is 'struck by its gloomy aspect, and eager to enter it'. A moment later, 'she began to talk with easy gaiety of the delightful melancholy which such a grove inspired'.

The melancholic frame of mind that characterized so much eighteenth-century poetry and so many hermitages was articulated through Milton's 'Il Penseroso'. Milton also contributed to the long line of architectural descriptions of the first hut, which was Adam's hut in the Garden of Eden. The hermitage in the paradisal garden has a complex history which has been ably charted by Joseph Rykwert in his learned book-length essay *On Adam's House in Paradise* (1972), which explores the idea of the primitive hut in architectural theory from Vitruvius to Le Corbusier and André Lurçat. Rykwert acknowledges that the existence of Adam's hut is an inference, as the Bible does not mention the accommodation in the Garden of Eden. He also regrets that because the plan of the first house has been lost, he is unable to outline its specifications. There is, however, no shortage of images of the second hut, the one that Adam and Eve erected after the expulsion. One image with which grand travellers might be familiar is the reed hut on the upper right panel of Ghiberti's 'Gates of Paradise', on the east doors of the Florentine Baptistery: in the upper left corner of the panel there is an image of Adam, Eve, and their two children in front of the hut. There is no image of the hut in which Adam (or, in the Protestant tradition, Adam and Eve) lived before the fall, but there is a description in Book IV of Milton's *Paradise Lost*. When Milton decides to tuck his Adam and Eve up for the night without pyjamas ('these troublesome disguises which we wear') he provides them with a 'shady lodge', an eco-hut which he designates as 'Adam's bower':

> the roof
> Of thickest covert was inwoven shade,
> Laurel and myrtle, and what higher grew
> Of firm and fragrant leaf; on either side
> Acanthus, and each odorous bushy shrub
> Fenced up the verdant wall; each beauteous flower,
> Iris all hues, roses, and jessamin

> Reared high their flourished heads between, and wrought
> Mosaic; underfoot the violet,
> Crocus, and hyacinth with rich inlay
> Broidered the ground, more coloured than with stone
> Of costliest emblem.

There was no death in Milton's unfallen Eden, so the floor could be embroidered with flowers that would never fade. The eighteenth-century root house is essentially Adam's bower accommodated to a fallen world in which patterned floors had to be made with stones or bones and living plants had to be replaced by dead but sturdy roots and chunks of wood. Adam's hut need not be waterproofed, as there was no rain in Eden (which had an underground irrigation system), but in the fallen world a sloped thatch roof was needed to keep the water out, as it is in modern Britain. This hut, for all its modesty, was the country house of our first parents, described in *Paradise Lost* as 'a happy rural seat of various view'.

One feature that sometimes occurs in Georgian hermitages is stained glass (most magnificently at Killerton), which seems oddly inconsistent with such modest buildings. The reason is once again to be found in Milton, in another passage in 'Il Penseroso':

> But let my due feet never fail
> To walk the studious cloister's pale,
> And love the high embowed roof,
> With antique pillars' massy proof,
> And storied windows richly dight,
> Casting a dim religious light.

The conventional image of the young Milton as a sour puritan cannot survive scrutiny of these lines. The cloisters, perhaps those of Westminster Abbey, are 'studious' because medieval Benedictine monks studied there. The young Milton admires the massive strength ('massy proof') of the pillars and is moved by the dim light that penetrates the richly decorated ('dight') stained glass windows. It is this passage that lies behind the anomalous appearance of stained glass in rustic hermitages.

At least three strands of eighteenth-century poetry help to explain the phenomenon of the garden hermit. One embodies the Horatian theme of solitary retirement to the countryside. The most popular example of this type of poem was 'The Choice', written in 1700 by John Pomfret, a Bedfordshire vicar. The poem, which is based on Horace's *Satire 6*, championed, as Dr Johnson explained, 'such a state as affords plenty and tranquillity, without exclusion of intellectual pleasures'. Johnson also testified to the popularity of the poem: 'perhaps no composition in our language has been oftener perused'.

The second genre that supports the notion of the hermit is the poetry of melancholy. The dark, reflective poems of the 'Graveyard Poets' were widely read. Thomas Gray's 'Elegy Written in a Country Churchyard' (1751), arguably the finest short poem in the English language, is still familiar to all students of English poetry, but nowadays only specialists read such once-popular works as Thomas Parnell's 'Night Piece on Death' (1721), Edward Young's 'Night Thoughts' (1742), and Robert Blair's 'The Grave' (1743). The works of these poets all evince a debt to Milton's 'Il Penseroso', and hermits are not uncommon in the literature of the period. Oliver Goldsmith's *Vicar of Wakefield* contains (in chapter 8) a ballad usually called 'Edwin and Angelina', which begins:

> Turn, gentle hermit of the dale,
> And guide my lonely way,
> To where yon taper cheers the vale,
> With hospitable ray

Similarly, Thomas Parnell's 'The Hermit' tells the story of a wandering hermit whose home was a cell:

> Far in a wild, unknown to public view,
> From youth to age a reverend hermit grew;
> The moss his bed, the cave his humble cell,
> His food the fruits, his drink the crystal well.

In Scotland, James Beattie's poem 'The Hermit' is set in a mountain cave where

> a Hermit began
> No more with himself or with nature at war,
> He thought as a sage, though he felt as a man.

The actress Mary Robinson, whose talent as a writer is too often occluded by her role as a royal mistress, retired from public life to become a poet and novelist. Her poems include 'Anselmo, the Hermit of the Alps':

> Deep in a forest's silent shade,
> For holy Meditation made,
> Anselmo lived!—his humble shed
> Reared, 'midst the gloom, its rushy head.
> Full many a flower, of loveliest hue,
> Around his mossy threshold grew;
> His little vineyard food supplied,
> His healthful cup the rippling tide;
> The wood his tranquil bower of noon,
> His midnight lamp the silvery moon;
> His simple garb and modest mien,
> The emblems of the soul within.

'Full many a flower' glances at Gray's 'Elegy' ('Full many a flower is born to blush unseen'), and the 'mossy threshold' reaches back to the 'mossy cell' of Milton's 'Il Penseroso'.

At least one writer anchored his imagination to the life of a real hermit. In 1771 Thomas Percy (later bishop of Dromore) published 'The Hermit of Warkworth', a long poem (800 lines) in the form of a ballad. Warkworth Castle and its hermitage, now in the care of English Heritage, are on the Northumbrian coast. The hermitage is on a river bank, and is accessible only by boat. It is a sandstone cave with a rib-vaulted chapel and residential accommodation for the hermit. The early history of the hermitage is unknown, but the architecture of the chapel implies that it was built in the late fourteenth century. The hermitage does not appear in any surviving record until 1487, when the hermit is named as Thomas Sharpe; his successors include John Greene (mentioned in 1506) and Edward Slegg (mentioned in 1515). The last hermit to inhabit the cave was one George Lancastre, to whom Henry Percy, the sixth earl of Northumberland, granted privileges on 3 December 1531. The hermitage is last mentioned in 1537, and 'George Lancastre priest' is named as the incumbent; it appears that he also had secular duties, because he is also described as the castle bailiff. In the eighteenth century, when several real hermitages were being reclaimed as social spaces, the hermit of Warkworth was appropriated by Thomas Percy (no relation to the earls of Northumberland) for his ballad. By this time there were two legends associated with the hermitage—that it was founded by one Bertram to atone for the murder of his brother, and that it was built by a soldier lamenting the loss of his beloved—and Percy combined the two in his tale. The poem proved to be immensely popular, and it survived the mockery of Dr Johnson to become an important force in the revival of medieval literature and in the shaping of popular ideas about hermits. One remarkable survival from the early nineteenth century, inspired by the poem or the actual hermitage, is a glass diorama box depicting the hermit (with cotton beard) beside his hermitage; it is now in private ownership in the United States.

The third poetic genre, and the one that most directly informs the idea of the hermit, was the verse inscription for the hermitage. The inscriptions of William Shenstone include this one for a hermitage:

> Fond man, to this sequestered cell
> Retire, and bid the world farewell
> Ah, quit the city's noisy scene
> For pleasures placid and serene,
> To find within this lone recess
> The rose-lipped cherub, Happiness,
> That haunts the hermit's mossy floor
> And simplest peasant's humble door.

Shenstone's inscriptions were to be accorded the honour of being translated into French for the garden at Ermenonville.

One of the most popular hermitage inscriptions was 'Father Francis's Prayer'. This is not the prayer popularly attributed to Francis of Assisi ('Make me an instrument of your peace; where there is hatred, let me sow love', etc.), which is an early twentieth-century invention, but rather a prayer composed by Gilbert West and attributed to Father Francis, the hermit of Mereworth Castle, Hawkstone, and Woodhouse. The prayer exists in several versions, of which these are the opening and closing lines, purged of West's attempt to mimic Chaucer's spelling:

> Ne gay attire, ne marble hall,
> Ne arched roof, ne pictured wall,
> Ne cook of France, ne dainty board,
> Bestowed with pies of Perigord,
> Ne power, ne such like idle fancies,
> Sweet Agnes grant to Father Francis.
> . . . .

> Right well I ween, that in this age,
> Mine house shall prove an hermitage.

This inscription was widely known because Robert Dodsley had included it in the fourth volume of his *Collection of Poems by Several Hands* (6 vols, 1748–58), which established the canon of mid-eighteenth-century poetry. Shenstone said in a letter that 'there is nothing I am more pleased with [in Dodsley's collection] than Father Francis's Prayer. Mr Berkley repeated it to me in my Root-house this last summer, and I think said it was Mr West's.' In 1750 West's inscription was accorded the honour of being published in a Latin translation by the poet and politician Nicholas Hardinge.

In some cases printed inscriptions constitute the only surviving evidence of the existence of a hermitage. William Cowper, for example, seems to have had a hermitage in his garden at Olney, where in May 1793 he addressed his 'Inscription for a Hermitage in the Author's Garden' to his companion Mary Unwin:

> This cabin, Mary, in my sight appears,
> Built as it has been in our waning years,
> A rest afforded to our weary feet,
> Preliminary to—the last retreat.

In 1758 Thomas Warton, the author of a poem on 'The Pleasures of Melancholy', visited Ansley Park, and there composed an 'Inscription in a Hermitage, at Ansley-Hall, in Warwickshire'; the poem, in four stanzas, begins:

> Beneath this stony roof reclin'd,
> I sooth to peace my pensive mind.

In 1804 the poet and priest William Lisle Bowles became vicar of Bremhill, in Wiltshire, and remodelled the gardens of the vicarage (now Bremhill Court) in imitation of Shenstone's garden at The Leasowes, adding personal touches such as sheep bells tuned to pleasing harmonies. His hermitage, unusually, had a religious dimension, in that it was a fanciful re-creation of the hermitage of St Bruno, the eleventh-century founder of the Carthusian Order. According to the *Gentleman's Magazine* (September 1814),

> proceeding directly up the slope from this place [the vicarage], you meet with a root-house Hermitage, with a rude stone table, a wooden chair, a small sun-dial on a fragment of a twisted column, and a rustic cross, which St Bruno, the Hermit, is said to have erected, and thus to have inscribed:
>
> > He who counted all as loss
> > Save peace, and silence, and the cross.

This is, as far as I know, the only emphatically Christian ornamental hermitage in Georgian England.

Hermits also feature in the prose fiction of the eighteenth century. The best known of these hermits are those in Fielding's *Tom Jones* and Dr Johnson's *Rasselas*. In the former, the eremetical Man on the Hill that Tom Jones and Mr Partridge encounter tells them his life story, a tale of a dissolute life that has led to his withdrawal from the world and a melancholic misanthropy; the novel is unsympathetic to this perspective, which it contrasts with Tom Jones's capacity for friendship. In the latter, Rasselas and his companions encounter a hermit in Egypt; his solitude is deemed to have removed him from temptation but not to have taught him anything about goodness.

With the emergence of the Romantic movement, the hermit began to receive more sympathetic treatment. This shift was apparent on the Continent as well as in Britain. Gotthold Lessing's poem *Der Eremit* (1749) presented a hostile view of the hermit. The emergence of Goethe, however, signalled a sympathetic treatment of the hermit and melancholic contemplation that was to influence understandings of the hermit in Britain. Hermits began to overrun German literature in the 1770s. Goethe's short satirical verse drama *Satyros oder Der vergötterte Waldteufel* ('Satyros, or the Idolized Demon of the Woods', composed 1773, published 1817) presents a kindly hermit with an instinctive understanding of nature. Similarly, Goethe's libretto for the singspiel *Erwin und Elmire* (performed 1776), modelled on Goldsmith's ballad of Angelina and Edwin in *The Vicar of Wakefield*, presents the hermit in his hut as a sympathetic figure. Jakob Lenz's dramatic fragment *Die Kleinen* (1775) and his novel *Der Waldbruder* ('The Friar of the Forest', 1776) idealize the withdrawal of the hermit from corrupting society. Friedrich Maximilian von Klinger's plays *Die Zwillinge* ('The Twins', 1776) and *Sturm und Drang* ('Storm and Stress', 1776) are dominated by the eremetical impulse, and the hermit is an important figure in his novel *Fausts Leben, Thaten und Höllenfahrt* ('Faust's Life, Deeds and Journey to Hell', 1791). Thereafter hermits populate a range of German plays, poems, and novels throughout the first half of the nineteenth century.

Hermits and other solitary figures also abound in the writings of the English Romantic movement, which was in significant part shaped by German Romanticism. Coleridge's *Rime of the Ancient Mariner*, for example, ends with the appearance of the hermit who lives in the woods by the shore. Similarly, Wordsworth's 'Tintern Abbey' evokes the image 'of some hermit's cave, where by the fire | The hermit sits alone', and *The Prelude* finds his thought drifting

> to other times,
> When, o'er those interwoven roots, moss-clad,
> And smooth as marble or a waveless sea,

Some hermit, from his cell forth strayed, might pace
In sylvan meditation undisturbed.

This passage is set in France, and it evokes Ariosto and Tasso, so on one level it is recalling real hermits, but the meditation is sylvan rather than sacred, and so brings to the mind of the reader the hermit of the English romantic imagination.

The architectural context

The idea of the primitive hut that is true to nature is deeply embedded in western cultures. In America, Abraham Lincoln famously travelled from a log cabin to the White House, and it is still possible to visit the Lincoln Log Cabin in Illinois. In fact Lincoln was working as a lawyer in Springfield when his parents moved into the log cabin in 1837, and the log cabin now open to visitors is a reconstruction undertaken in 1935, but it nonetheless exerts a powerful grip on the American imagination, even though the log cabin in which Lincoln was born was in Kentucky, not Illinois. Similarly, the utopianism of American transcendentalist writers, whose ideals included subsistence farming, achieved an architectural embodiment in Thoreau's one-room cabin at Walden Pond, which is now regarded as the birthplace of the American conservation movement; the replica cabin has become a pilgrimage destination. The apogee of the European version of the primitive hut is the Palladian villa, which at its most extravagant is a small palace in the countryside, but is nonetheless understood as a restoration of Adam's hut. Such buildings gesture at our wish to be connected with our rural origins as surely as the modern second home in the countryside, the cottage with central heating and air conditioning; for those who cannot afford a cottage, there is the economical alternative of a house number mounted on a piece of knotty pine.

In this context the hermitage in the garden represents more than whimsy or ephemeral fashion, but is a gesture towards our origins in an edenic log cabin and towards the ideal of the simple life. The hermitage, like the replica log cabin, is a reconstruction of the primitive hut in paradise, just as the garden is an attempt to create the paradisal state. The landowner with the requisite sensibility was a man of feeling, and in some cases, notably that of Mrs Delany, the female designer of the garden could be a woman of feeling. The hermitage and its corporeal or imagined hermit represented the sympathy of the person of sensibility for the natural world, and the emotional insights afforded by melancholic withdrawal. Such sentiments make it easy to understand why the landowner sometimes chose to become his own hermit.

The hermit and the hermitage are the shabby successors of the comfortable pastoralists of the seventeenth century. When in the mid-seventeenth century Robert Herrick (in 'To Phillis') offered pastoral gifts to the imaginary lady of his heart's affections, he insisted that the quality of the gifts would ensure that no one mistakes her for a real shepherdess:

> I'll give thee chains and carcanets
> Of primroses and violets.
> A bag and bottle thou shalt have,
> That richly wrought, and this as brave;
> So that as either shall express
> The wearer's no mean shepherdess.

Pastoralism in such poems is a genre for well-scrubbed aristocratic ladies and gentlemen; the sheep never have ticks. Similarly, portraitists such as Sir Peter Lely revived an aristocratic pastoral idiom in which ladies posed as shepherdesses with hair arranged in hurluberlu coiffures and dresses remarkable for their bold scoop décolletage. In the eighteenth century this type of pastoral fell out of fashion, and the fashion for the garden hermit arose out of the more naturalistic pastoralism that followed. Primitivist impulses could no longer accommodate the love-sick swain wooing his shepherdess, and modulated into the classical ideals of Horatian retirement and the contemplative 'happy man' of Virgil's *Georgics*. The hermit and his hermitage thus became a representation of the aspiration to the simple life, the life of rural retirement characterized by philosophical and scientific curiosity. The garden hermit embodied both the primitivist vision and the Enlightenment ideals of curiosity and the examined life.

One of the most striking features of the shift from the seventeenth-century appropriation of classical pastoral to the pastoral values that underlie the phenomenon of the garden hermit is the relative roles of men and women. In the seventeenth century the pastoral figure is often (but not always) an aristocratic woman. In the eighteenth century, the real or imagined hermit was a man, but hermitages were often the creations of women, including Queen Caroline, Princess Elizabeth (daughter of George III), Lady Luxborough, Lady Acland, Lady Hertford, Lady Rolle, and the immensely influential Mrs Delany, all of whom will be discussed in the pages that follow. Did the real or imagined figure of the silent hermit in the garden somehow embody the contemplative aspirations of the women who commissioned the hermitages? Even in cases such as the earl and countess of Orrery, it is striking that it was Lord Orrery who commissioned the hermitage but Lady Orrery who articulated the contemplative ideal of the hermit. This is not a subject on which it is wise to be dogmatic, but it seems clear that there is a gender dimension in the phenomenon of the garden hermit.

The decline of the hermit

By the early nineteenth century, the garden hermit was going out of fashion. Why should this be so? One answer may be the rise of abolitionism: in at least one instance, at Hawkstone, the position of the hermit came to be regarded as analogous to that of the slave, and the substitution of a stuffed hermit for a living one was said to have been prompted by 'the popular voice against such slavery [, which] had induced the worthy baronet to withdraw the reality and substitute the figure'. It seems, however, that the hermit survived the abolitionist movement, because there was still a hermit at Hawkstone in the early twentieth century.

A more likely reason for the decline of the hermit was that the eighteenth-century ideal of pleasing melancholy was fading, as was the related cult of sensibility. Dr Johnson had complained about 'the fashionable whine of sensibility'. A little later, Horace Walpole's essay *On Modern Gardening* (1780) was a harbinger of what eventually became a widespread view:

> the Doric portico, the Palladian bridge, the Gothic ruin, the Chinese pagoda, that surprise the stranger, soon lose their charm to their surfeited master.... But the ornament whose merit soonest fades, is the hermitage, or scene adaptable to contemplation. It is almost comic to set aside a quarter of one's garden to be melancholic in.

The fashion for sensibility could not survive such censure indefinitely, and as the cultivation of strong emotions abated, so their expression in the hermit in the woods faded. The figure of the hermit disappeared, and in the Victorian period the hermitage moved out of the woods onto the lawn, where it became a garden feature. The garden hermit lived on in attenuated form, and in the final chapter I will outline how the ornamental hermit and his hermitage have persevered through changing fashions to re-emerge in the twenty-first century.

3

The Hermits

It is now impossible to ascertain how many Georgian country houses had hermitages, and how many of those hermitages were furnished with hermits, because much of the evidence has been lost. Indeed, some of the surviving evidence is so vague that it cannot be verified. One such example appeared in 1924 in an article by Osbert Sitwell published in *Criterion*:

> At one great house in England the accounts disclose a half-yearly pay-
> ment of £300 to a hermit, who had, for this commensurate salary, to
> remain bearded and in a state of picturesque dirtiness for six months
> in the year in an artificial cave at a suitable distance from the house—
> just far enough (but not too far) for the fashionable house-party, with
> its court of subservient poets and painters, to visit, walking there in
> the afternoons, peering into the semi-darkness with a little thrill of
> wonder and excitement.

Alas, the house is not specified, but the account cannot be dismissed out of hand, because Osbert Sitwell was the younger brother of Edith Sitwell, who was to write an important essay on 'Ancients and Ornamental Hermits', and so knew the phenomenon well. Fortunately many other hermits can be given a local habitation, if not a name.

There were several sorts of hermits inhabiting garden hermitages. The most common type was the imaginary hermit, whose presence was indicated by furnishings, and temporary absence by objects such as eyeglasses or a book left on the table; the habitation of these hermits will be discussed in Chapters 4 and 5. This chapter will deal with corporeal hermits. These were mainly hired hermits, but in other instances, the landlord (or in one case, the landlord's brother) could be his own part-time hermit. Finally, the hermit could be a stuffed or wooden figure.

The job market

Securing the services of an ornamental hermit for one's hermitage was not easy, so landowners advertised. Similarly, at least one aspiring ornamental hermit took out an advertisement with a view to securing employment, and another wrote to a prospective employer to see if a post could be created for him. There is evidence of at least six advertisements, of which I have been able to find only one; the others may have taken the form of handbills. These six include one Scottish advertisement, for which the evidence takes the form of an entry in the *Table Talk* of the Romantic poet Samuel Rogers:

> Archibald Hamilton, afterwards duke of Hamilton (as his daughter, Lady Dunmore, told me) advertised for 'a hermit' as an ornament to his pleasure grounds; and it was stipulated that the said hermit should have his beard shaved but once a year, and that only partially.

Archibald Hamilton became the ninth duke of Hamilton, and his daughter Susan became countess of Dunmore. As the ninth duke acceded to his dukedom in 1799, the advertisement must have been circulated before that date. His pleasure grounds were at

Hamilton Palace, in Lanarkshire (built 1695, demolished 1921). It is not known whether Lord Hamilton managed to recruit a hirsute hermit.

Our knowledge of three advertisements is grounded on a note by 'Florence' (from Dublin) that appeared in Notes and Queries in 1852. Florence's identity is uncertain, but the redoubtable bookman Ian Jackson, who has unrivalled expertise in the pseudonyms of *Notes and Queries*, has suggested (in response to my query) that the Irish poet, translator, and Young Irelander Denis Florence MacCarthy would be a distinct possibility. MacCarthy is arguably the most talented of those Irish poets who have entirely disappeared from popular consciousness and are remembered only by specialist historians. The combination of a Dublin address, the middle name of Florence, a habit of using pseudonyms in essays (Desmond, Vig, Trifolium, Antonio), previous contributions to *Notes and Queries* (under pseudonyms), picturesque antiquarian interests, and occasional references to hermits in his poetry (such as 'Where the fugitive found shelter, became the hermit's cell' and 'some from their hidden haunts remote, | Like him the lonely hermit of the hills') mean that the evidence all points in the same direction, but that constitutes likelihood rather than proof.

As the advertisements that Florence cites could not be traced, I wondered whether they might be fakes. I was particularly suspicious of this one, which was said to have appeared in *The Courier* on 11 January 1810:

> A young man, who wishes to retire from the world and live as an hermit in some convenient spot in England, is willing to engage

with any nobleman or gentleman who may be desirous of having one. Any letter addressed to S. Lawrence (post paid), to be left at Mr. Otton's No. 6 Colman's Lane, Plymouth, mentioning what gratuity will be given, and all other particulars, will be duly attended to.

My difficulty, apart from the inherent improbability of someone aspiring to become an ornamental hermit, was that there was no Colman's Lane in Plymouth in 1810. Eventually, however, I found the advertisement amongst the small ads on the front page of one of the many newspapers that used the title *Courier*, and realized that Florence's transcriptional errors included substituting 'Colman' for 'Colmer'. There was indeed a Colmer's Lane in Plymouth, and in the early nineteenth century its residents, who included a solicitor, a mason, a brewer, and a tobacconist, were accused of 'throwing great quantities of filth and dirt into the street'. Neither S. Lawrence nor Mr Otton appears in these records as a thrower of filth and dirt, so we do not know whether Mr Lawrence ever secured a hermitage; perhaps he is still waiting.

Florence's second advertisement is the most problematical of the three. He records that

Mr Powyss, of Marcham, near Preston, Lancashire, was more successful in this singularity: he advertised a reward of £50 a year for life, to any man who would undertake to live seven years under ground, without seeing anything human: and to let his toe and finger nails grow, with his hair and beard, during the whole time. Apartments were prepared under ground, very commodious, with a cold bath, a chamber organ, as many books as the occupier pleased, and provisions served from his own table. Whenever the recluse wanted any convenience, he was to ring a bell, and it was provided for him. Singular as this residence may appear, an occupier offered himself, and actually staid in it, observing the required conditions for four years.

There is no hint of the form in which this advertisement appeared, nor, as a correspondent of *Notes and Queries* pointed out (3 April 1852), is there a place called 'Marcham' near Preston. As 'Florence' wrote from Dublin, his English geography may have been as weak as his transcriptional skills. I think that the first sentence should have read 'Mr Powys, of Atherton Hall, near Bolton, Lancashire'. Atherton is not particularly close to Preston (40 km), nor is it called Marcham (which is a village in Oxfordshire), but Atherton Hall (near Bolton) had passed by marriage to the Powys family in 1726. In 1797 Thomas Powys was ennobled by Pitt as Baron Lilford; he died in 1800, but his descendants lived in the house until it was demolished in 1824. It would seem to have been a member of this family who secured the services of a subterranean hermit. The grounds of Atherton were in part absorbed into what is now a public park in Leigh. Somewhere beneath that land a hermit may once have lived, reading and occasionally ringing for cave service. As he had no human contact, he was hardly ornamental, though the chamber organ may have made him audible.

The terms of this advertisement seem bizarre, but in part they seem to have represented the standard job specifications. A letter from an aspiring hermit (discovered in 2003) mentions similar terms. The letter was almost certainly addressed to the Honourable Robert Drummond (seventh son of the fourth Viscount Strathallan), who in 1772 bought Cadland Manor, on the edge of the Solent in Hampshire. Four years later he embarked on the construction of a new house and landscape park, so the unsigned and undated letter must have been written after 1776. The spelling of the original is semi-literate (e.g. 'nown for human Cind'), so I have transcribed it in modern spelling:

Honoured Sir,

I have taken this freedom to acquaint your honour it is to as a favour as never yet was known for human kind to do that if your honour pleases to build a small hut as a hermitage near your honour's house in a wood with a high wall round it your honour might hear of a man to live in it for seven years without seeing any human creature that is to see [say?] what nature would turn to in that time I mean not to cut my hair nor yet my beard nor my nails in that time I should wish to have all necessities of life brought to me in a private place without seeing anybody and if your honour will give proper encouragement for them years I would.

There are very considerable similarities to the Atherton Hall advertisement, and some of the differences are minor: a hermit behind a high wall would be as invisible as one accommodated underground. Nigel Temple, who found the letter, assumed that there was no hint of remuneration, but I take the phrase 'proper encouragement' to be a request for payment. The speculative applicant for the Cadland Manor post included in his letter a sketch of the sort of hermitage that he thought would be suitable, and explained that he would disclose his identity when construction was under way. There is no evidence that a hermitage was ever built, so the hopeful hermit was almost certainly disappointed in his expectations.

Florence's third advertisement is also untraceable, but in this case there is ample supplementary information available, because the advertiser was the proprietor of Painshill (Surrey), which is well documented. The Honourable Charles Hamilton was the fourteenth child and youngest of the nine sons of the sixth earl of Abercorn. As a younger son he did not inherit an estate, and on his father's death in 1735 Hamilton secured a position at court through the influence of his sister Jane (Lady Archibald Hamilton), who was the companion (and possibly mistress) of Frederick, Prince of Wales. Hamilton became member of parliament for Truro and receiver-general for Menorca (which had been ruled by the British since 1708), but when the island fell to the French in 1756, and Admiral Byng was famously executed on the quarterdeck of the *Monarque*, Hamilton lost his income. He was, however, compensated with a secret service pension of £1,200 a year. In 1738, Hamilton had begun to buy heathland near Cobham, in Surrey. It was this land that he transformed into Painshill Park, which by the time he was forced by reduced financial circumstances to sell it in 1773 had been extended to more than 250 acres (100 hectares).

Painshill is the earliest major garden of the picturesque movement. It was designed as a series of landscape pictures that would provoke different sensations and emotional responses in its visitors. A garden driven solely by ideology can be boring, as any visitor to the old Soviet Parks of Culture and Rest can attest, but Painshill commands the interest of any student of historic gardens. Painshill had in Charles Hamilton a knowledgeable and imaginative designer who was supremely talented, and the result is a garden that retains its distinctiveness in the galaxy of great European gardens.

The paths of Painshill led the visitor through a sequence of contrasting scenes which were differentiated by setting, garden buildings, and the colours of foliage. One of these garden buildings was a hermitage which was set in a stand of firs in a distant corner of the park. Visitors approached, as the politician and writer Thomas Whately recorded, by a path that was overhung and dark. Another visitor, the Irish politician John (later Sir John) Parnell, wrote after a visit in 1763:

> You come to the top of a little eminence where you strike into a wood of different firs, acacia, etc, and serpentising through it arrive at an hermitage formed to the front with the trunks of fir trees with their

bark on, their branches making natural Gothic windows. The first room is furnished with a little straw couch, an old table and a few old chairs; in the back room are a parcel of odd old things, and from it you command a pretty view of the country. It is built on the side of a steep hill, so has another cave under its back apartment where you come to after several windings.

The hermitage was constructed on a mound. In Parnell's account, the 'upper apartment' was 'supported in part by contorted legs and roots of tree, which formed the entrance to the cell'. This description is consistent with a drawing, now in the Bodleian Library in Oxford, by the German landscape artist Friedrich Ludwig von Sckell, who visited in the garden in the mid-1770s. It was for this hermitage, in Florence's account, that Mr Hamilton had sought an ornamental hermit:

> Mr Hamilton, once the proprietor of Payne's Hill, near Cobham, Surrey, advertised for a person who was willing to become a hermit in that beautiful retreat of his. The conditions were, that he had to continue in the hermitage seven years, where he should be provided with a Bible, optical glasses, a mat for his bed, a hassock for his pillow, and hour-glass for his timepiece, water for his beverage, food from the house, but never to exchange a word with the servant. He was to wear a camlet robe, never to cut his beard or nails, nor ever to stray beyond the limits of the grounds. If he lived there, under all these restrictions, till the end of the term, he was to receive seven hundred guineas. But on breach of any of them, or if he quitted the place any time previous to that term, the whole was to be forfeited. One person attempted it, but a three weeks' trial cured him.

The advertisement has never been found, and until recently there has been no serious evidence that there was ever a hermit at Painshill. The research of Jan Clark, a Painshill volunteer, however, has uncovered both the name of the hermit and evidence for the existence and content of the advertisement. On Christmas Day 1773 the

FIGURE 3.1 Friedrich Ludwig von Sckell, drawing of Painshill hermitage.

London Evening Post included in 'Postscript' (a miscellany column) this notice:

> One Remington, now in St George's hospital, has undertaken for 500£ to live for seven years in a cave, in Mr Hamilton's garden, near Cobham in Surrey; during which time no person is to see him except Mr. Hamilton. He is to have all the necessities of life, but is not to be shaved, not to cut his nails, nor his hair during the whole time.

This was clearly an old story, as Charles Hamilton had sold Painshill earlier in the year, but it does give a name, and it does corroborate several of the details in Florence's account. As patient records for St George's only survive from 1781, the trail goes cold with the hermit's surname—but at least we know that Mr Remington the hermit existed.

The terms of this advertisement are recalled in a 'Curious Anecdote' recounted in the *Public Advertiser* on 17 June 1788, and it would

seem that either this or an earlier version on which it is based constituted Florence's source:

> the late owner Mr Hamilton advertised for a person who was willing
> to become the hermit of that retreat, under the following among
> many other conditions: that he was to dwell in the hermitage for
> seven years; where he should be provided with a Bible, optical glasses,
> a mat for his bed, and a hassock for his pillow, an hour-glass f[o]r his
> time-piece, water for his beverage from the stream that runs at the
> back of his cot, and food from the house, which was to be brought him
> daily by a servant, but with whom he has never to exchange one syl-
> lable; he was to wear a camblet robe, never to cut his beard or his nails,
> to tread on sandals, nor ever to stray in the open parts of the ground,
> nor beyond their limits, that if he lived under all these restrictions till
> the end of his term, he was to receive seven hundred guineas; but on
> breach of *any one* of them, or if he quitted his place any time previous
> to that term, the whole was to be forfeited, and all his loss of time
> remediless. One person attempted it, but three week [*sic*] were the
> utmost extent of his abode.

This is the fullest surviving account of the advertisement, and yet it
hints that there are even more conditions than those specified here.
It would seem that either Hamilton produced a very long advertisement, possibly in the form of a handbill, or that details of a
shorter advertisement have been elaborated in the retelling. In this
version the stipend has been raised from £500 to £700, but in other
particulars it is consistent with the earliest account. Subsequent
versions of the story have the hermit being caught in the local tavern after three weeks and dismissed, and more recent elaborations
include improper relations with a dairy maid. This was clearly a
hermit who was expected to dress like one: he was required to be
barefoot ('never tread on sandals'), like a Discalced Franciscan
('discalced' means 'without shoes'), and his uniform consisted of a

camblet (i.e. woollen) robe, possibly to evoke associations with the costume of druids.

In 1777 John Fuller, who is popularly but inaccurately known as Mad Jack Fuller (he seems to have been wholly sane), inherited from his uncle the family estate of Rose Hill, in Brightling (Sussex). After a tumultuous political career, in the course of which he defended the living conditions of plantation slaves (he owned a plantation in Jamaica) and was ejected from the House of Commons for drunkenness, Fuller left parliament at the dissolution of 1812 and settled at Rose Hill, where he had already embarked on the construction of a memorable set of follies. He began with a Coadestone (i.e. ceramic) summer house with a 'Tudor' arch (restored 1992) and went on to commission his own mausoleum (an 8-metre high pyramid in Brightling churchyard), a rotunda garden temple, an obelisk known as the Needle, a hermit's tower and a building known as the Sugar Loaf (an 11-metre cone which alludes to his sugar plantation).

The 8-metre hermit's tower was built with a view to accommodating an ornamental hermit, and Fuller is said to have advertised for a hermit, with the usual conditions of service. Here, for example, is the account in *Follies: A National Trust Guide*:

> The requirements were a little excessive: no shaving, no washing, no cutting of hair and nails, no conversation with any outsider for a period of seven years, after which the happy hermit would be made a Gentleman. No takers.

I have not been able to trace the advertisement. The reason for this failure, I think, is that there was no advertisement. Fuller's follies are enigmatic, and myths have emerged from the fog of uncertainty. Fuller is said, for example, to be interred in his pyramid sitting at a table dressed for dinner, with a bottle of claret awaiting consumption. In the same way, the tower, which may have been a viewing platform for Bodiam Castle (which Fuller owned and restored), is now known as the hermit's tower. It has been expertly restored by the British Gypsum Company, and tourists can climb to the top to enjoy the view, but Fuller's intention to accommodate a hermit in the building is a harmless fantasy devised long after his death.

Finally, there are two cases of hermits being sought in the Lake District. Joseph Pocklington, the son of a wealthy banker in Nottingham, built a serious of houses in the English Lakes. In 1778 he bought Vicar's Island, on Derwentwater; he renamed the island Pocklington's Island, and it is now known as Derwent Island. In the course of clearing the island of trees in order to construct his 'improvements', Pocklington discovered a large stone that he declared to be part of a druids' temple. He then reconstructed the temple, using as a model the genuine stone circle at nearby Castlerigg. He built a house on the island (now in the care of the National Trust), and then began to build on land that he acquired on the Ashness shore of the lake. The most ambitious of these buildings was Barrow Cascade House (or Barrow House), on which work began in 1787; this building survives, and is now a youth hostel. In the grounds Pocklington built a hermitage, of which a sketch survives in the Cumbria Record Office. It is a Gothic building that resembles a chapel, and indeed has a bell mounted on the top of the façade. Pocklington hoped to install a hermit in the building, and offered the generous rate of half-a-crown a day, but no suitable candidate was willing to submit to the disciplines that he required, which, in the account of Sir William Gell's *A Tour in the Lakes Made in 1797*, stipulated that

> the hermit is never to leave the place, or hold conversation with any-one for seven years during which he is neither to wash himself or cleanse himself in any way whatever, but is to let his hair and nails both on hands and feet, grow as long as nature will permit them,

In the same period, Pocklington acquired the Borrowdale land that contained the Bowder Stone (now on National Trust land), and enhanced its surroundings by erecting a new druid's stone and a small hermitage; this hermitage was too small to accommodate a resident hermit, so Pockington's hermitages both remained unoccupied.

Elsewhere in the Lake District, at Conishead Priory (Cumbria), Colonel Thomas Richmond-Gale-Braddyll, may have enjoyed more success. In 1821, the year in which he served as High Sheriff of Lanca-shire, Colonel Braddyll (as he was known) ordered the demolition of the house that had replaced the Augustinian priory, and commis-sioned Philip Wyatt to replace it. The hermitage on the nearby hill was probably one of the follies built by Wyatt, but may have been built on the foundations of a hermitage associated with the medieval priory. The building consisted of a cell to accommodate the hermit, and an adjoining chapel.

The Conishead hermitage was the subject of a report to the Cum-berland and Westmorland Antiquarian and Archaeological Society in 1902. In response to this report, a member of the Society (Harper Gaythorpe) submitted additional information:

> Dr. T. K. Fell, of Barrow-in-Furness, tells me that about 1868 the Her-mitage had a little stained glass in a small window, and there were the remains of ruins of other buildings near. Before then, Dr. Fell's father remembered (so he told him) that about 1820 Colonel Braddyll kept

an old man as a hermit at the Hermitage. He was there for about 20 years, during which time he never had his hair or nails cut. Dr. Fell's father recollected the old man, who came from Bardsea, and the Colonel kept him as a curiosity.... Mr. Coward, of Ulverston, one of our members since 1884, also says that Col. Braddyll kept the hermit as a sort of show....

Mr. Gaythorpe suggests that some time after 1821, when Colonel Braddyll had the artificial gable erected on Chapel Island, he had this Hermitage made habitable for his sham hermit, and that the weather-beaten blocks of limestone of which the cell is built may have been obtained from the grotto.

The transmission of oral evidence renders it difficult to evaluate, because narratives develop as they are retold, but it is distinctly possible that Colonel Braddyll kept a hermit. Bardsea is not the Welsh island associated with druids (now spelt Bardsey), but rather a fishing village near Conishead Priory. The religious dimension implied by the presence of a chapel is certainly unexpected, but is not inconsistent with the idea of melancholic reflection. Conishead Priory is now the home of the Manjushri Kadampa Meditation Centre, so the tradition of meditation carries on.

Hawkstone and Woodhouse

Hawkstone Park, near Shrewsbury, is the creation of successive generations of the Hill family. Hawkstone Hall is largely the work of the diplomat and public servant (Lord of the Treasury from 1699 and a Lord of the Admiralty from 1702) Richard Hill. His nephew Sir Rowland Hill (first baronet) began the creation of a picturesque landscape garden, and this process was triumphantly concluded by Rowland's son, Sir Richard Hill (second baronet), who succeeded his father in 1783. Sir Richard is best known as a fiery Methodist controversialist who defended Calvinism against the Arminianism of John Wesley. His resolute Protestantism led in 1795 to his erecting a 30-metre monument (which still dominates the estate) to his sixteenth-century ancestor Sir Rowland Hill, whom Sir Richard declared to be the first Protestant mayor of London. There is no shred of evidence to suggest that this Sir Rowland was a Protestant, but mere facts do not stand in the way of celebrating one's ancestors. In the face of Hill's anti-Catholic prejudice, it is pleasing to report that Hawkstone Hall is now a Roman Catholic retreat.

The setting of the garden was ideally suited to Sir Richard's ambition to create a wild landscape, the most dramatic features of which are integrated into red sandstone cliffs. It still looks sufficiently wild to have been used to represent Narnia in the BBC version of C. S. Lewis's fantasy novels, and the surviving follies are now a popular tourist attraction. The tradition of welcoming the public extends back to the eighteenth century: there were ten editions of *A Description of Hawkstone, in Shropshire, the Seat of Sir Richard Hill, Bart* by an otherwise unknown 'T. Rodenhurst' (presumably a pseudonym, possibly for Sir Richard Hill) between 1783 (when it had 19 pages) and 1811 (70 pages and eight plates), and in 1790 Hill opened the Hawkstone Inn to accommodate visitors.

In the second edition Rodenhurst described the hermit (a 'solitary sire') and a

> well-designed little cottage, which is an hermit's summer residence. You pull a bell, and gain admittance. The hermit is generally in a sitting posture, with a table before him, on which is a skull, the emblem of mortality, an hour-glass, a book and a pair of spectacles. The venerable bare-footed Father, whose name is Francis, (if awake) always rises up at the approach of strangers. He seems about 90 years of age, yet has all his senses to admiration. He is tolerably conversant, and far

from being unpolite, and, if requested, will repeat the following lines, which are fixed up in the inside of his habitation:

> Far from the busy scenes of life
> Far from the world, its cares and strife,
> In solitude more pleased to dwell
> The hermit bids you to his cell:
> Warns you sin's gilded baites to fly,
> And calls you to prepare to die.

Father Francis continued to seem 'about 90 years of age' through successive editions of the guidebook.

Nothing is known of Father Francis save that he had the secret of eternal age and only worked in the summer. There is some evidence, however, that Father Francis was from time to time replaced by a stuffed hermit. Sir Richard Colt Hoare, who had inherited Stourhead in 1785, visited Hawkstone on 28 July 1801. He approvingly noted 'the figure dressed up as a Druid' in the grotto, but was not as enthusiastic about his encounter with the stuffed hermit, despite its ability to move and speak. He describes a hill on which there is

> a building wherein is the figure of a hermit who moves and speaks. The face is natural enough, the figure stiff and not well managed. The effect would be infinitely better if the door were placed at the angle of the walk, and not opposite you. The passenger would then come across St Francis by surprise, whereas the ringing the bell and door opening into a building quite dark within renders the effect less natural.

The figure seems to have been an automaton, though how it moved and spoke is not known. Automata were certainly fashionable in the late eighteenth century, and there were many developments arising from Jacques de Vaucanson's defecating duck of 1739 (which was driven by a clockwork mechanism), including Wolfgang van Kempelen's attempts in the 1770s and 1780s to produce artificial speech.

In Hoare's account, Father Francis has become St Francis, which offers a clue to the perception of both the living and the stuffed hermits. Francis of Assisi had introduced the eastern practice of going bare-footed into the western church, so Hill's Father Francis was bare-footed. Indeed, the title 'father' is indicative of fictional membership of one of the orders of mendicant friars, perhaps in his case the Discalced Franciscans. It may seem highly unlikely that an anti-Catholic polemicist like Sir Richard Hill would have a benign religious understanding of St Francis, but Calvinists have long had a soft spot for St Francis, of which the clearest manifestation is the work of Paul Sabatier, the Calvinist scholar and pastor at Strasbourg whose biography of St Francis (1893) evinced a deep sympathy for the ideals of St Francis and the Franciscans. Indeed, fictions such as the one at Sir Richard Hill's hermitage are an important stage in the evolution of St Francis from a stern and passionate saint to the New Age notion of Francis as a medieval hippie who retreated to the woods to commune with nature and play with the animals.

Another account of the automaton occurs in the diary of Thomas Martyn, who visited Hawkstone with his wife and son in the autumn of 1801 (the year of Hoare's visit):

> We were now conducted to the hermit's cell, which is certainly the best representation of what the poets describe that I ever saw. You ring a bell and the door immediately opens of itself and discovers a venerable bare-footed old man seated in a recess with a table before him, on which is a skull, an hour glass, a book and a pair of spectacles; he rises as you approach and bows. On your putting questions to him, his lips move, and he answers in a hoarse hollow voice, coughs as if almost exhausted. He told us that he was 100 years of age, and that he had resided there the greatest part of his life. Over the recess was 'Memento mori' in large letters, but there being some other lines which I could not make out for want of light, he was asked if he could repeat them, and he expressed himself as follows

Far from the busy scenes of life,
Far from the world, its cares and strife,
In solitude more pleased to dwell,
The hermit bids you to his cell;
Warns you Sin's gilded baits to fly,
And calls you to prepare to die.

The deception is admirable. The gardener, who is invisible, must be the actor, and an admirable one he is. The naked feet are well carved, and so is the face, for although the eyes and lips move and the figure rises, it is certainly a mere automaton. Over the door is written 'Procul O procul esti Profani'.

The Latin phrase (which means 'Keep away, keep away, O uninitiated ones') is taken from Virgil's *Aeneid* 6.258; the words are spoken by the priestess who is to guide Aeneas in the underworld as she excludes the uninitiated from the ritual. The same phrase is inscribed on the Temple of Flora at Stourhead. The description of the hermitage as 'the best representation of what the poets describe' is eloquent testimony to the debt of the hermit and his hermitage to the literary tradition.

Another source of information about the Hawkstone hermit is a satire in which it is difficult to separate fact from fiction. From 1822 to 1835 *Blackwood's Edinburgh Magazine* carried a series of 71 imaginary conversations set in the Edinburgh tavern of a man called William Ambrose, and hence called the *Noctes Ambrosianae* ('Nights at Ambrose's', with a pun on 'ambrosian', with reference to the food of the gods). More than half of these were written by John Wilson, who represented himself as a character called 'Christopher North' in dialogues characterized by scurrilous and very funny exchanges. In the April 1830 edition of the magazine, *Noctes Ambrosianae* took the form of a conversation which concludes with an exchange between Christopher North and the 'Shepherd'

(James Hogg, whose Scots idiom is wonderfully captured in the *Noctes*).

NORTH: By the bye, the Editor of the Monthly Review is a singular person....

SHEPHERD: O the coof! Wha is he?

NORTH: For fourteen years, James, he was hermit to Lord Hill's father.

SHEPHERD: Eh?

NORTH: He sat in a cave in that worthy baronet's grounds, with an hour-glass in his hand, and a beard once belonging to an old goat—from sunrise to sunset—with strict injunctions to accept no half-crowns from visitors—but to behave like Giordano Bruno.

SHEPHERD: That's curious. Wha had the selection o' him—think ye?

The dialogue presents several puzzles to the modern reader. The *Monthly Review* was an English journal which was published from 1749 to 1845. As a correspondent of *Notes and Queries* pointed out on 15 May 1852, 'this is certainly strange training for a future editor'. The editor of the *Monthly Review* in this period was the Irish journalist Michael Joseph Quin, whose Catholicism may have made him a target for satire about a hermit. In any case, the description of the hermit with whom the editor is satirically associated has some elements of truth, in that the Hills had a hermit who (in Rodenhurst's account) was equipped with an hour-glass. The beard that once belonged to an old goat is a new detail, as is the injunction to behave like Giordano Bruno, the Italian Dominican friar who was burnt for heresy in 1600. I have stood before Bruno's statue in Campo dei Fiori (in Rome) and wondered how best to behave like him, but to no avail. In the nineteenth century (when the statue was made) Bruno came to be regarded as a martyr to the advancement of science, in part because his view that the sun was a star had been vindicated, but also because of the pantheist strain in his thought. The final puzzle is the reference to the cave. In other accounts the hermit's habitation is said to be a cottage, but there is an engraving from the 1780s depicting the hermitage as a cave. Perhaps this was a hermit with two residences.

Yet another account of the Hawkstone hermit appears in John Timbs's *English Eccentrics* (1875):

> In 1810, a correspondent of *Notes and Queries*, visiting the grounds at Hawkstone, the seat of the Hills, was shown the hermitage there, with a stuffed figure dressed like the hermits of pictures, seen by a dim light; and the visitors were told that it had been inhabited in the daytime by a poor man, to whom the eccentric but truly benevolent Sir Richard Hill gave a maintenance on that easy condition; but the popular voice against such slavery had induced the worthy baronet to withdraw the reality and substitute the figure.

Again, details of the account ring true, but there is a problem, in that *Notes and Queries* was not founded until 1849. The answer to this little puzzle is that the date is wrong, and that the note that John Timbs cites was published in *Notes and Queries* on 18 December 1852; it was written by the clergyman and historian Henry Walter, a regular contributor during this period, and a reliable witness. His note takes us as close as we are likely to get to an understanding of the ornamental hermit of Hawkstone.

And what of Father Francis's successors? Despite abolitionist sentiment, the post of hermit at Hawkstone was apparently hereditary, and was for generations held by a family called Jones. One hermit called Jones, disporting a fine wig and false beard, was photographed standing in the doorway of his hermitage behind a table with a skull. An inscription overhead begins 'Procul O' before disappearing into

FIGURE **3.2** The Hawkstone hermit.

the thatch. A second photograph, apparently of a slightly later date, survives in the Shropshire Archives in Shrewsbury.

In 1895 the third Viscount Hill went bankrupt, and in 1915 the Hawkstone estate was sold off in 131 lots. One of the buildings on the estate (not the main house) became the Hawkstone Park Hotel, which retained the services of a hermit. Barbara Jones, the historian of follies and grottoes, asserted in 1953 that the Hawkstone hermit must have existed well into this century, as Miss Cynthia Adburgham remembers that when she was a child visitors paid to tour the grounds and the hotel employed a hermit who sat in a cave fondling a skull; he must have been the last hermit.

I have not been able to identify Miss Cynthia Adburgham, but the period that she was recalling is clearly the early twentieth century. Perhaps this Mr Jones was the last hermit, but as late as 1983 an elderly Mr Jones from the same family was acting as a guide at the estate, though without a hermit's uniform. The hermitage with the Virgilian inscription was destroyed by fire in March 2008, but a new hermitage has been constructed on the same site.

Father Francis, the hermit of Hawkstone, also had a residence at Woodhouse (now spelt Wodehouse), the estate of Sir Samuel Hellier

FIGURE 3.3 The new hermitage at Hawkstone.

at Wombourne, in Staffordshire. This was one of a closely related set of Midlands gardens that will be discussed in the next chapter. Woodhouse was distinguished from its neighbours by the presence of a hermit. In an ornamental woodland above the house, Sir Samuel placed a suite of follies, including a hermitage in a paled enclosure. In 1765 the antiquary and traveller John Loveday described the hermitage as

> curious indeed, consisting of several apartments, moss and roots the material; by springs the hermit, formed very naturally, has motions that surprise his visitants, who suppose him inanimate.

The hermit was clearly an automaton. A watercolour of 1773 shows the hermit standing by an altar in the chapel. The room in the foreground contains the hermit's bed and a stool. On the wall above

FIGURE 3.4 The interior of the hermitage at Woodhouse, with Father Francis.

the stool, 'Father Francis's Prayer' is painted on a plaque. The text must have been taken either from a printed source or from the original at Mereworth Castle. The mechanical hermit is thus identified as Father Francis.

Francis was represented in a wholly benign light at Hawkstone, Woodhouse, and Mereworth. Such was not the case at Medmenham, where another Francis presided.

Medmenham and Tong

Sir Francis Dashwood was chancellor of the exchequer, but is better known for his founding of the aristocratic society variously known as the Friars of St Francis of Wycombe or the Franciscans or the Medmenham Monks. The group is popularly known as the Hellfire Club, but this name arises from confusion with an earlier (and similarly debauched) club founded by Philip Wharton, duke of Wharton. In 1751, Dashwood secured the ruins of the Cistercian Abbey at Medmenham, on the Thames near Henley, and added a ruined tower and a small cloister to make the atmosphere suitably Gothic. Walpole visited in 1763 (as a tourist, not a participating member) and commented that 'the nymphs and the hogsheads [of wine] that were laid in against the festivals of this new church, sufficiently informed the neighborhood of the complexion of those hermits'. Walpole was refused admission to the obscenely decorated chapel where the friars conducted mock-Catholic ceremonies, but did see the living quarters, noting that friars 'meet to drink, though the rule is pleasure, and each is to do whatever he pleases in his own cell, into which they may carry women'. This was not a typical hermitage, but rather one, as Walpole observed, dedicated to Venus and Bacchus. This same theme characterized Dashwood's garden at West Wycombe (now in the care of the National Trust), where he created an erotic landscape with a Temple of Venus and a Mound of Venus. The mound was decorated with erotic statues, and at its base had an entrance with a suggestive shape; as the politician John Wilkes (one of the Friars of St Francis) explained, the opening 'is the same entrance by which we all come into the world and the door is what some idle wits have called the door of life'. The vulgarity of the Friars, the Hooray Henrys of the eighteenth century, knew no bounds. In the Victorian period the Temple of Venus was demolished, but in 1982 Sir Francis Dashwood, the eleventh baronet, commissioned a reconstruction based on archival and archaeological evidence, so the Temple can once again be seen. Medmenham Abbey is now a private residence.

It is possible that Tong Castle, in Shropshire, hosted a provincial version of the Friars of St Francis. The obituary notices published in the October 1822 issue of the *Gentleman's Magazine* record the death in Shropshire on 6 October of 'C. Evans, better known by the name of Carolus the Hermit of Tong, where he had lived during seven years in a lonely and romantic cell on the domain of G. Durant, Esq'. Tong Castle was a Gothic country house built in the early 1760s by George Durant (now best known as the lover of Lady Lyttelton of Hagley Hall) and demolished in 1954. It seems to have been hung with pictures that gave offence to visitors: the diarist John Byng, later fifth Viscount Torrington, recorded in 1792 that the paintings of 'dying saints, naked Venuses, and drunken bacchanals' constituted an 'offensive show, disgusting to every English eye that has not been hardened in Italy'. 'Why', he asked, 'produce savage and indecent exhibitions before your children's eyes?' Durant died in 1780 and was succeeded by his four-year-old son (also George Durant), who was one of the children that Byng had in mind.

When the younger George Durant came into his inheritance in 1797, he began to populate the gardens of Tong Castle with follies. The spirit in which these follies were constructed is hard to judge, because they seem to edge beyond the picturesque and to hint at some darker purpose. Crosses were carved in walls, and a pulpit (half demolished by vandals in the 1970s and now overgrown) modelled on the magnificent refectory pulpit now in the grounds of Shrewsbury Abbey was mounted on a garden wall. One house in the gardens was Rosary Lodge, and another at the top of Tong Hill was called The Priory. A building called Convent Lodge (part of the ruins of a non-existent nunnery) had a portress who dressed as a nun. An iron seat under a tree in the garden was known as St Swithun's chair, with reference to the episcopal seat of the ninth-century bishop of Winchester. When Swithun's relics were translated to Winchester Cathedral on 15 July 971, there was heavy rainfall (hence the popular belief that rain on St Swithun's Day portends forty days of rain). The Tong St Swithun's chair was in fact a water-toy: guests who sat on the chair triggered a mechanism that poured water on them from pipes hidden in the tree. The ecclesiastical follies, the 'nun', and the watery chair all recall the calculated blasphemy of Sir Francis Dashwood's Friars of St Francis. Durant was a notorious womanizer who fathered many illegitimate children with estate servants, and the surviving evidence points to Tong as a venue for debauchery and mock-Catholic ceremonies similar to those at Medmenham.

It is in this context that Carolus the ornamental hermit must be considered. George Griffiths, the unreliable Victorian chronicler of Tong, argued that the building known as the Hermitage was

> so called from the fact that a miserable poor half-witted man once chose to live in a cave-like place cut in the rock behind it. He dressed himself in a kind of coarse cloth, and wore a long white untrimmed

beard. He is said to have been a gentlemen who had seen better
days.... For several years he chose to inhabit this dismal cave.

Griffiths had seen the obituary notice in the *Gentleman's Magazine*
(though it is imperfectly transcribed), and it is clear that in his understanding Charles Evans was a man who had fallen on hard times
rather than one who had been employed as an ornamental hermit. It
seems possible, however, that Griffiths misunderstood the purpose
of the hermit and misrepresented his hermitage. The physical
appearance of the hermitage is apparent in two watercolours that
survive in the Shropshire archives. The evidence for the hermit is
contained in two additional paintings, only one of which survives.

Carolus was evidently regarded as a 'character', and his portrait was
painted by William Armfield Hobday, a highly fashionable painter
who at one stage averaged six sitters a day. His most famous painting
was his portrait of Charles Evans entitled *Portrait of Carolus (lately
Deceased, Distinguished as the Hermit of Tong Castle, Shropshire)*,
which was exhibited at the Royal Academy in 1823, at the British Insti-
tution in 1824, and at Hobday's Gallery of Modern Art in 1829. When
Hobday failed financially, the painting was listed among his assets,
but thereafter it disappeared, and has never been recovered. Fortunately, a description of the painting was included in the memoir of
Hobday published in *Arnold's Library of Fine Arts* in 1831:

> If, as it is said, genius is more felicitous at one time than another, cer-
> tain it is that Hobday while at Broad Street painted a picture, the like
> of which he never did before nor after; viz. the painting known as the
> *Hermit of Tong*, an individual passing under the name of Carolus, liv-
> ing on the estate of Colonel Durant in Staffordshire [an error for
> Shropshire]. This work is distinguished by a fine subdued brilliancy in
> the flesh, depth and transparency in the shadows, and great harmony
> of colouring in the whole. It represented the Hermit at the mouth of

his Hermitage, the left elbow resting on a book and hand raised to the temples; the back part of his head was enveloped in a hood, and the transparency of its shadow on the upper part of the head was particularly clear, rich, and well painted, and the folds of his dark brown habit were broad and easy. Altogether this was undoubtedly his *chef-d'oeuvre*. Many were the applicants for its purchase; but, with all its excellencies, no one would give the moderate sum he fixed, of 100 guineas; and this likewise went, like all his other effects, at the sale.

The portrait was posthumous, and so may not have been true to the features of the hermit, but it is quite clear that Carolus was portrayed as an ornamental hermit with habit and hood.

There the matter rested until 2007, when Robert Jeffery published *Discovering Tong*, which has a wealth of new material, including a colour insert of hitherto unknown watercolours from the sketchbook of George Durant the younger, including one of the hermitage and the hermit. The hermitage is a stone 'ruin' on a wooded slope at the foot of a waterfall. The bearded hermit, who stands in front of his hermitage with a walking staff, wears a russet tunic and a brown broad-brimmed hat, which is the traditional dress of the pilgrim to Rome or Santiago de Compostela. If we are right to think of Durant's Tong as a provincial version of Dashwood's hedonistic Friars of St Francis, then the hermit may not be as innocent a figure as he seems to be in the painting.

The death of Carolus created a vacancy which was later filled for a brief period by James Guidney, a former army drummer (his drum is in Fort York, in Toronto) who moved into the hermitage. In the event he only lasted for a month (11 June–11 July 1825) before embarking on a new career as Jemmy the Rockman, walking the streets of Birmingham selling from a tin canister his 'composition', a cough remedy in the form of a sweet. A watercolour portrait in the Birmingham

Art Gallery shows a man with a long white beard holding a canister (which also survives in the Birmingham collection), so Guidney had the hirsute appearance requisite in an ornamental hermit. According to his autobiography, he lost an eye on service in Malta, and had a vision of a lamb in the form of a man who instructed him to wear a beard thereafter. Clearly the lamb was preparing Guidney for his short career as a hermit.

The perversions of both the religious and the secular ideals of the hermit embodied in the practices of Medmenham and, it seems, at Tong are unhappy reminders of a degenerate aspect of eighteenth-century life. It comes as a relief to turn to the wholesome civilities of the White brothers at Selborne.

Gilbert White at Selborne

Gilbert White's *Natural History of Selborne* is a book that has charmed generations of readers, including me. I came to the *Natural History* through *Portrait of a Tortoise* (1946), an edition by the poet and novelist Sylvia Townsend Warner of the passages in which White describes the behaviour of his tortoise, who was called Timothy. In the event, the tortoise's gender identity proved to be problematical, for Timothy was eventually revealed to be female. I have on my wall an engraving of her successor at Selborne, also called Timothy; in a gentle irony of history, this second Timothy also turned out to be female.

White's house (which was called 'The Wakes') in the Hampshire village of Selborne is now a museum, and commemorates Gilbert White and two members of the Oates family: the ornithologist Frank Oates and his nephew, Captain Lawrence Oates of the Antarctic.

White's property was not an estate, but the garden was capacious (seven acres, supplemented by part of a neighbour's orchard), and had some of the features of much larger gardens, including a grassed terrace with a sundial, a turfed 'mount' (an artificial mound) from which to view the garden, a two-dimensional Hercules designed to create the illusion of a large statue, and a ha-ha that facilitated views of countryside which included large oil-jars on pedestals. To these features White added a hermitage that became the focal point of his entertaining in clement weather, and he later added a second hermitage. Many of the eighteenth-century features have now been restored, but they do not include these hermitages.

The artefacts in the museum include the original manuscript of *The Natural History and Antiquities of Selborne*, which was first published in 1788 and has seldom been out of print (though the part on antiquities is not usually reprinted). *The Natural History*, which was fashioned from White's diaries and correspondence, was destined to shift the starting point of natural history from the study of specimens to the study of the living world. His account (17 August 1768) of the discovery of the three types of what he called 'willow-wrens' and we know as 'leaf-warblers', for example, begins with the assertion that he has 'now, past dispute, made out three distinct species of the willow-wrens... which constantly and invariably use distinct notes'. In distinguishing the three species (now known as chiffchaff, willow warbler, and wood warbler) he also attends to habitat: the wood warbler, for example, 'haunts only the tops of trees in high beechen woods, and makes a sibilous grasshopper-like noise now and then, at short intervals, shivering a little with its wings when it sings'. It is these observations that lead White to 'the specimens of the three sorts now lying before me', and his anatomical examinations confirm the distinctions that initially arose from his observation of living birds.

Birds eat worms, and White's hymn of praise to the earthworm (20 May 1777) shows in its opening sentences why he is regarded as the founding father of biodiversity:

> earthworms, though in appearance a small and despicable link in the chain of nature, yet, if lost, would make a lamentable chasm. For, to say nothing of half the birds, and some quadrupeds, which are almost entirely supported by them, worms seem to be the great promoters of vegetation, which would proceed but lamely without them, by boring, perforating, and loosening the soil, and rendering it pervious to rains and the fibres of plants, by drawing stalks of leaves and twigs into it.

Never has the humble earthworm been so honoured. The *Natural History of Selborne* was rightly destined to become one of the progenitors of the genre of books that chronicle the rhythms of the English countryside.

What is the place of the garden hermit in the mind of a man whose garden occasions reflections on the taxonomy of the warbler and the wonders of the earthworm? The illustrations in the first two editions of the *Natural History of Selborne* afford some sense of White's thinking. The engraved title-page does not portray a warbler or a worm, but rather shows a hermitage and its hermit, beneath which is written 'where the hermit hangs his straw-clad cell'. The phrase comes from Gilbert White's 'Invitation to Selborne', in a passage in which he assures the visitor that

> The Muse shall lead thee to the beech-grown hill,
> To spend in tea the cool, refreshing hour,
> Where nods in air the pensile, nest-like bower;

Or where the Hermit hangs the straw-clad cell,
Emerging gently from the leafy dell;
By fancy plann'd.

The image in the oval is a detail from a watercolour by Samuel Hieronymous Grimm now hanging at Dunham Massey, a National Trust
property in Cheshire (see Plate 4). The painting has preserved the
appearance of both hermitage and hermit. The figure of the hermit
is not marginal to the *Natural History of Selborne*, but is central to
White's understanding of the contribution that sympathetic humans
can make to the natural world. The hermitage in this image, with its
surmounted cross, bears a distinct resemblance to those pictured in
Sadeler's prints. This was the first of White's two hermitages; its less
exotic successor can be seen on the frontispiece to the *Natural History*, which is a view of Selborne in which the second hermitage
appears high on the hill known as the Hanger.

The story of the hermit and the two hermitages can be tracked
through the letters and journals by any reader sufficiently resolute to
ignore the warblers and earthworms. The hermitages were built
twenty years apart, in 1756 and 1776. Costs were met by subscription, apparently from family members (unless reminders of unpaid
subscriptions are a family joke). The first hermitage had the familiar
lines from Milton's 'Il Penseroso' inscribed over the door ('May at
last my weary age | Find out the peaceful Hermitage, | The hairy
gown and mossy cell'). The hermit is revealed as Gilbert's youngest
brother Harry, the Reverend Henry White, whose day job was that of
rector and schoolmaster at Fyfield, near Andover. He was, like Gilbert, a naturalist and diarist, but he also happily donned the costume
of a hermit to entertain Gilbert's guests while they munched on the
cantaloupe that he grew in his garden. It is unfortunate that his six

surviving volumes of diaries, now divided between the Bodleian Library and the British Library, only begin in 1780, after Henry had retired as a hermit, so there is no extant diary of an ornamental hermit.

The journal of 20-year-old Catherine Battie (daughter of the eminent physician William Battie), who spent the summer of 1763 with her two sisters at Selborne, offers some recompense for the loss of Henry's early diaries. She records that on 24 June 'we went back to the Hermitage to tea [and] in the middle of tea we had a visit from the Old Hermit; his appearance made me start. He sat some time with us and then went away.' An entry from Gilbert's diary written a month later (28 July) records an occasion in which the guests participated in a pastoral fiction:

> Drank tea twenty of us at the Hermitage: the Miss Batties and the Mulso family contributed much to our pleasures by their singing, and being dressed as shepherds and shepherdesses. It was a most elegant evening, and all parties appeared to be highly satisfied. The Hermit appeared to great advantage.

The entries in both diaries throughout the summer record pastoral festivities with the hermit in sociable attendance. In the autumn the Miss Batties had to leave, and Harry the hermit rose to the occasion with an elegy entitled 'Daphne's Departure':

> Too plain my heart forbodes that fatal hour,
> When dearest Daphne leaves the happy vale;
> Let then this breast own Love's resistless power,
> Nor longer strive its anguish to conceal.
>
> The hoary hermit in his calm retreat,
> No longer safe from her resistless charms;
> With trembling hand, dim eye, and faltering feet,
> Sighs out his dotage o'er her snowy arms!

Not to be outdone, Gilbert composed a poem called 'Kitty's Farewell to the Stump Beneath the Hermitage', and his poem contains a detailed description of his brother the hermit:

> Kitty, a grateful Girl, in doleful dump,
> On the steep cliff deplored her favourite stump.
> 'Shall I no more (the melting maiden cries)
> With thy sweet scenes delight my feasting eyes:
> Say, shall no more thy nearer views engage,
> The crowded tent and swelling Hermitage;
> Shall the cowled sage no more my sight beguile,
> So stout, yet so decrepit all the while;
> Wondrous old man, in whom at once combine
> The hoary hermit, and the young divine
> In dapper hat adorned, and pastoral dress,
> Must I forget each sister shepherdess;
> While amorous swains, bending with anxious care,
> Down the loose slope conduct their sliding fair.

It was clearly a golden summer.

Thereafter the profile of the Selborne hermitage remains low until 1776. Many minds were preoccupied with the explosion of the American Revolution, but at Selborne the brothers were preoccupied with the construction of a new hermitage. On 27 May Gilbert wrote to his brother Thomas to say, 'we have finished the hermitage, and I desire to know what I am to charge you towards it, as you were so kind as to make a tender of your subscription'. Thomas sensibly declined to answer, so on 24 June Gilbert sent a chasing letter: 'if you don't write soon and forbid me, I shall set you down as a subscriber to the Hermitage, which is finished'. The only description of this second hermitage at the point of its construction occurs in a letter written by Gilbert to Samuel Barker on 1 July 1776.

> We have built a new Hermitage, a plain cot[tage]: but it has none
> of the fancy, and rude ornament that recommended the former to
> people of taste: this is strong and substantial, and will stand a long
> while, fire excepted.... Bro[ther] Harry made me a visit, and was
> much delighted with what was going on; and in particular with a view
> of the hermitage, which Grimm is to copy for him in town.

Grimm's watercolour portrayed Harry in front of the original hermitage. This is the picture that passed through Harry's descendants
(the earls of Stamford) and thence to Dunham Massey.

Harry died in 1788, and Gilbert followed him to the grave five
years later. The last journal entry in which Gilbert mentions the hermitage (1 December 1791) notes an improvement: 'the Hermitage,
now capped with a coat of thatch, and embellished with a large cross,
makes a very picturesque object on the Hanger, and takes the eye
agreeably'. These may have been hermitages from which crosses pro-
truded, but the diary entries make it clear that they had little to do
with Christianity. They were, as Gilbert says, 'picturesque'. The diary
entries make it clear that social occasions that took place at the hermitage were characterized by an air of pastoral frivolity rather than
one of sanctity. The White brothers and their guests became partici-
pants in a picturesque scene, figures in the garden at the centre of the
landscape.

The fashion for garden hermits ended with the death of King George
IV, but there was an attenuated survival into the Victorian era at
Vauxhall Gardens, on the south bank of the Thames. These gardens,
which were for two centuries the best-known of London's pleasure
gardens, were opened in 1661, and a hermitage was constructed in
their wooded north-east corner in 1757. The hermit was in the first

instance represented by a painted figure shown reading a book, but in 1821 the Gardens changed hands, and the new owners revamped the hermitage and installed a live hermit. The hermitage, which was constructed of wood and canvas, was at the end of a dark walk. It had a painted interior that created the illusion of the interior of a hermit's hut. The resident hermit was a fortune-teller, and often featured in accounts of the gardens. An engraving of 1832 depicts the hermit in his cottage being visited by a young gentleman. An account of such a visit is included in Thackeray's *Vanity Fair* (1848), in which a lonely Captain Dobbin decides not to join any of the groups of couples:

> 'I should only be *de trop*,' said the Captain, looking at them rather wistfully. 'I'd best go and talk to the hermit,'—and so he strolled off out of the hum of men, and noise, and clatter of the banquet, into the dark walk, at the end of which lived that well-known pasteboard Solitary. It wasn't very good fun for Dobbin.

The hermit was a real person, but is here associated with his pasteboard surroundings, which were described in greater detail by the German traveller Max Schlesinger, whose stroll through the gardens took him to a gloomy avenue, 'which leads us straight-way to *Fate*, to the hermit, and the temple of Pythia...in the guise of a gipsy'. The gipsy's accommodation is simple, but

> the dwelling of the sage hermit is much less primitive, nor are believers permitted to enter it. They must stand on the threshold, from whence they may admire a weird and awful scenery—mountains, precipices and valleys, and the *genius loci*, a large cat with fiery eyes, all charmingly worked in canvas and pasteboard, with a strict and satisfactory regard for the laws of perspective. The old man, with his beard so white and his staff so strong, comes up from the mysterious depth of a pasteboard ravine; he asks a few questions and disappears again, and in a few minutes the believer receives his or her Future,

THE HERMIT OF VAUXHALL.

A BALLAD, AFTER OLIVER GOLDSMITH.

BY THE EDITOR.

" Turn, gentle hermit of Vauxhall,
    And let me know the way
In which, within that cavern small,
    You pass your time away.

" There 's nothing but a little lamp,
    A pitcher, and a cat ;
The place must be extremely damp—
    Why don't you wear a hat ? "

" No chaff, my son," the hermit cries,
    " But walk your chalks along ;
Your path to the rotunda lies—
    They 're going to sing a soug."

Figure 3.5 The hermit of Vauxhall.

carefully copied out on cream-coloured paper, and in verses, too, with his or her name as an anagram. Of course these papers are all ready written and prepared by the dozen, and as one lady of our party had the name of Hedwig—by no means a common name in England—she had to wait a good long while before she was favoured with a sight of her fate. This, of course, strengthened her belief in the hermit and the fidelity of her husband.

In 1845, *Punch* printed a light-hearted report of the rumours 'that Vauxhall Gardens are going to be built upon' and 'that the Hermit is to be knocked down by public auction'. Four years later the popular writer (and famous mountaineer) Albert Richard Smith alluded to the persistent talk of closure, noting that the end of summer always brings whispers of 'Vauxhall being "built upon"' but that 'as Whitsuntide comes round, we find that Vauxhall springs up again' and

> the hermit returns to life—I wonder what becomes of him at Christmas, and if he employs all the winter months in writing the fortunes he distributes in the summer ones.

The most jaundiced view of the hermit came from the journalist and novelist Edmund Hodgson Yates, who described Vauxhall Gardens as 'a very ghastly placc' where 'of actual garden there was no sign'. He noted with dismay a range of tawdry attractions which included 'a hermit in a false beard, dwelling in a "property" cave [i.e. a cave furnished with props], who told fortunes'. He said of Vauxhall that 'the aristocracy had deserted it, and no wonder'. In 1859 the Gardens closed, the hermit lost his job, and builders moved in. The buildings on the site now include the headquarters of MI6, where the false beards of the hermit of Vauxhall may live on.

Marginal hermits

Collectors of ornamental hermits have found that their numbers are disconcertingly few, and so have included inadvertent hermits, self-declared hermits, and recluses. The last category includes people who were clearly mad, and deserve compassion rather than treatment as amusing lunatics, and so are not treated here. Inadvertent and self-declared hermits, however, are a marginal category: all were associated with gardens, but none was employed by a landowner.

The irascible travel writer and self-publicist Philip Thicknesse is perhaps the clearest example of a self-proclaimed hermit. In 1774 Thicknesse sold his house in Bath's fashionable Crescent and moved his family to a cottage in nearby Bathampton. He constructed a small hermitage in the garden, making decorative use of human skeletons that were dug up in the garden. Two years later he embarked with his wife and six of his eight children on a journey through France and Spain; the family's pet monkey, Jacko, was dressed in a red jacket and boots, and rode postilion. The high point of the journey was an inspirational visit to the hermitages and convent of Montserrat—the same complex that had inspired King Philip IV to build the hermitages of Buen Retiro. Thicknesse did not have the resources to build a palace, but when he arrived back in Bathampton he renamed his cottage as the Hermitage of St Catherine in affectionate remembrance of L'ermita de Santa Caterina at Montserrat. In the garden he erected a memorial to Thomas Chatterton beneath which he interred Anna, his eldest daughter. Shortly thereafter his two sons inherited fortunes from their maternal grandfather, the sixth earl of Castlehaven. The younger son, Philip Thicknesse, bought the Hermitage of St Catherine from his father, and so ended Philip Thicknesse's eremetical period. In his memoirs Thicknesse refers repeatedly to his delightful hermitage, and insists that he has 'obtained that which every man aims at but few acquire; solitude and retirement'. He declines a request from a friend to describe his hermitage, and does not discuss his life as a hermit, but does observe that

> The duplicity of Mankind, and satiety of enjoyments all tend to show
> that even the splendid scenes, which surround the palaces of wealth

and greatness, are never thought complete, unless marked by some
shady cave and the abode of an imaginary anchorite.

Thicknesse seems to have been his own imaginary hermit.

Some strands of the literature on follies promote the view that they
were commissioned by beneficent landowners to provide work for
their tenants at times of hardship. Perhaps so (or perhaps not), but it
is clear that landowners did not scruple to remove entire villages if
their landscape gardeners declared the villages to be a blot on the
paradisical landscape. In 'The Deserted Village' Oliver Goldsmith
describes one such eviction from the fictional village of Auburn:

> But now the sounds of population fail,
> No cheerful murmurs fluctuate in the gale,
> No busy steps the grass-grown footway tread
> But all the bloomy flush of life is fled—
> All but yon widowed, solitary thing,
> That feebly bends beside the plashy spring;
> She, wretched matron, forced, in age, for bread,
> To strip the brook with mantling cresses spread,
> To pick her wintry faggot from the thorn,
> To seek her nightly shed, and weep till morn,
> She only left of all the harmless train,
> The sad historian of the pensive plain.

It is distinctly possible that Auburn is modelled on the Oxfordshire
village of Nuneham Courtenay, which was shifted to a new site in the
early 1760s to enhance the view from the house. If so, the 'wretched
matron' who was left behind was modelled on Babs Wyatt, an elderly
widow who remained in the garden till her death. She became, in the
view of the Harcourts and their visitors, an Arcadian shepherdess, a

point of interest on the circuit of the garden. This pastoral fantasy does not make Mrs Wyatt an ornamental hermit, but shares with that phenomenon a tendency to reduce real people to figures in the landscape.

William Lole, who lived in the Leicestershire village of Newton Burgoland (near Ashby-de-la-Zouch), described himself as a hermit and spent his days in his garden. In a report in Robert Chamber's *Book of Days* dated 1863 Lole is described as 'an eccentric character' who

> lives among the haunts of men, in a comfortable cottage; he can enjoy a good dinner, can drink his glass of beer, and smoke his pipe with as much relish as any man. Yet, according to his own definition, he is entitled to the appellation of a hermit. 'True hermits', says he, 'throughout every age, have been the firm abettors of freedom'. And, as regards his appearance, his fancies, and his habits, he is a hermit—a *solitaire*, in the midst of his fellow-beings. He wears a long beard, and has a very venerable appearance.... He has no less than twenty different kinds of hats, each of which has its own name and form, with some emblem or motto on it.

At the end of a long description of the hermit's clothing, the account ends with an assurance that Lole has chosen to spend his life wearing emblematical clothing in his garden. His brother offered to accommodate him, 'but "No", says the old hermit, "for what would then become of my garden? My heart is in my garden. I cannot leave it".' This sentiment is common all over Britain, but it is not normally articulated by a self-declared garden hermit.

4

The Hermitage in Georgian England

The garden hermitage, with its attendant ideology of melancholy, is a phenomenon bound by place and time. The place is Britain and Ireland, though the English garden sometimes carried with it a hint of its ideology when exported to the Continent. The time is the Georgian period, which is the century from the accession of George I in 1714 to the death of King George IV in 1830. Thereafter hermitages continued to be built, but they were simply ornamental garden buildings. I shall turn to an English example of a Victorian hermitage at the end of this chapter, and to a Scottish example at the end of the next chapter.

The British and Irish hermitage tends to take one of two forms: the root house or the architectural hermitage. Few of the former survive, because wood is less durable than stone, but in this chapter I have also taken account of lost root houses; in a few cases, I am able to reproduce images of these lost buildings.

The question of what constitutes a garden hermitage is not always easy to answer. Georgian gardens had buildings with a variety of names, including grottoes, gazebos, pavilions, root houses, and hermitages. The distinctions between these types of buildings are not always clear-cut. A grotto is an artificial cave that imitates the natural caves which in classical antiquity were deemed to be the home of nymphs and water deities. This supernatural association survived the transition to Christianity, and throughout the Christian era grottoes have had spiritual associations. Grottoes were introduced into gardens in sixteenth-century Italy, and were typically decorated with pebbles, moss, and seashells. In France, grottoes were accommodated in artificial hills, and the hermitage at Gaillon is in this sense a grotto. This overlap between grotto and hermitage also occurred in England: Pope's grotto at Twickenham enabled the poet to withdraw from the world to an environment that had been associated with the muses since antiquity. A gazebo is quite distinct from a grotto, but can overlap with a hermitage. The word seems to be a jocular Latinism: just as lavabo (Latin: I shall wash) came to refer to a basin, so gazebo (mock-Latin: I shall gaze) was coined to refer to a place from which a garden could be viewed. Some ornamental hermitages were hidden in woodlands, but others were constructed, like gazebos, to afford a view for the hermit and his guests. A folly (an unnecessarily harsh term) is a garden building that has been included for design purposes rather than for utility. It traditionally takes the form of a tower (often a ruined tower), but temples, eye-catchers, obelisks, pavilions, gazebos, and hermitages can also be follies. A garden pavilion, which may be enclosed or unenclosed, is distinguished from similar buildings by its purpose, which is to provide a sheltered setting for entertainment. A root house is a type of hermitage constructed or decorated with gnarled roots, but some root houses are not hermitages. In many cases the defining characteristic of a hermitage is the presence of a real or imagined hermit, but even that idea is problematical, because a few grottoes had hermits. Similarly, some buildings designated as druids' cells (including Henry Hoare's at Stourhead) were also called hermitages.

This survey of Georgian garden hermitages is compendious rather than complete; the sole evidence for many hermitages lies hidden in estate archives, and may never be found. There were large numbers of hermitages, and at the height of their popularity in the mid-eighteenth century, most landscape gardens seem to have had a hermitage tucked away in woodland. In a few cases the presence of a hermitage in the garden is indicated by the main house being called 'The Hermitage', but that name normally has a different origin. The idea of the hermitage as a place of secular retirement (described in Chapter 1) gradually percolated down to the middle classes, and eventually virtually any house could be designated as a hermitage. Registers of listed buildings include scores of eighteenth-century houses called 'The Hermitage'. In Mayfield (Staffordshire), for example, the fine house known as 'The Hermitage' has a lintel inscribed 'Wm Bott in his Old age Hath Built him an Hermitage 1749', so designating William Bott's place of retirement; paradoxically, there is a late Georgian root house in Mayfield, but it seems to have been designated as a summer house rather than a hermitage. 'The Hermitage' is also the name a country house on the River Tyne near Acomb (Northumberland), so called because it was built on the reputed site of the eighth-century hermitage of John of Beverley (actually an oratory to which he retreated from official business). One of the outbuildings has a graffito that reads 'D DAVIS 1785 HERMITAGE', which could mean that there was a Georgian hermitage here, but seems more likely to mean that the carver was registering his presence at the house called 'The Hermitage'.

Some hermitages were designed by landowners or their landscape architects. It was also possible, however, to take or adapt a design from one of the numerous folly pattern books published in the mid-eighteenth century. Perhaps the best known is William Wrighte's *Grotesque Architecture Or Rural Amusement: Consisting Of Plans, Elevations, And Sections For Huts, Retreats, Summer And Winter Hermitages* (1767), which was last reprinted in 2010. Wrighte's plans include seven hermitages: a simple Hermitic Retreat made from roots and irregular branches, a Hermit's Cell (with rustic seating alcoves and a skull surmounting the door), an Oriental Hermitage (with an inscription in a faux-Arabic script), a Winter Hermitage ('intended as a retirement from hunting, fowling, or any other winter amusement'), a Summer Hermitage (with a floor 'paved with sheeps marrowbones placed upright'), an Augustine Hermitage (with wings that end in pavilions to accommodate a library and a bath), and a Rural Hermitage (with a gazebo on the roof).

The European court hermitage was immensely influential in Britain, but the form of British hermitages was altogether different, because the buildings, whatever their architectural form, were exceedingly modest. In gardens meant to imitate the Garden of Eden, the simplicity of the hermitages gestured towards Adam's hut in Paradise. The first ornamental court hermitage appeared in an English garden in the early 1730s, built at Richmond for Queen Caroline (George II's consort) to a design by the architect and landscape designer William

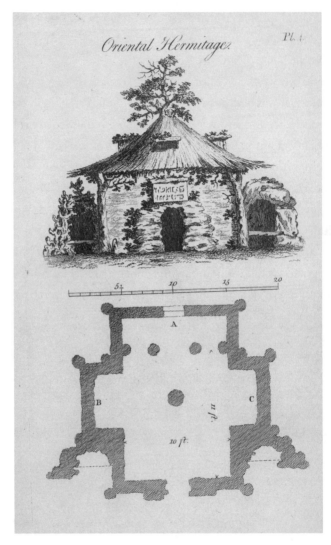

FIGURE **4.1** William Wrighte, design for Oriental Hermitage.

Kent. The Queen had a great passion for gardens. She commissioned the extension and landscaping of Kensington Gardens, and the lake known as the Serpentine in Hyde Park. At Richmond she commissioned royal gardens linked by a walk through a 'forest' to Kew. The Queen was an advocate of the 'natural' school of garden design, and saw her role 'in helping nature, not losing it in art'. These gardens all contained buildings, of which the two that attracted most contemporary comment were designed by William Kent for Richmond: the Hermitage and Merlin's Cave. These buildings were used to promote the British credentials of King George II and his consort Queen Caroline, both of whom were Germans.

FIGURE 4.2 Hermitage designed by William Kent for Queen Caroline, Royal Gardens, Richmond. Wash drawing attributed to Bernard Lens III.

Construction of the Richmond hermitage began in November 1730. The site was in what is now the Royal Botanic Gardens at Kew. The hermitage was built as a 'ruined' building topped by a small bell-tower, and was set in front of an artificial hill with trees and shrubs. The three parts of the façade consisted of a pedimented central section and two wings, all constructed from roughly cut stone. Each of the three sections had an arch fitted with a gilt-iron railing. Inside there was an octagonal room with niches for busts. The building was the work of three considerable figures: it was designed by Kent, supervised by the architect Henry Flitcroft, the royal clerk of works, and built by Andrews Jelfe, a masonry contractor who later built the first Westminster Bridge (demolished 1852 when the present bridge was built). Like eminent architects and builders now, their services were not cheap: the total cost of the hermitage was £1,375, an absurdly inflated sum. The appearance of the hermitage was described by Nicholas Amhurst (writing as 'Caleb D'Anvers') in *The Craftsman* (13 September 1735, reprinted immediately in the *Gentleman's Magazine*). He described it as

> a heap of stones, thrown into a very artful disorder, and curiously embellished with moss and shrubs, to represent rude nature. But I was strangely surprised to find the entrance of it barred with a range of costly gilt rails, which not only seemed to show an absurdity of taste, but created in me a melancholy reflection that luxury had found its way even into the hermit's cell.

The central railing was a gate, and as the bookseller Edmund Curll recorded after a visit in 1736, 'a person attends to open the gate to all comers'. In a court hermitage one would expect no less.

The sculptor Giovanni Battista Guelfi fashioned four marble busts (John Locke, Isaac Newton, Samuel Clarke, and William Wollaston) for the Hermitage, and later added a bust of the natural philosopher Robert Boyle. The often repeated contention that there was a sixth bust (of Francis Bacon) is a myth, as is the notion the busts are the work of the sculptor Michael Rysbrack and that Guelfi only executed the terracotta models. In fact Guelfi sculpted both the terracotta models (later owned by William Kent) and the finished marble busts, and Rysbrack acknowledged that they were the work of Guelfi. The choice of English figures was intended to assert the Englishness of the new German monarchs. All five subjects were associated with science or natural religion (Clarke and Wollaston are now obscure, but were then well-known figures in moral and natural philosophy), which were disciplines in which English dominance was being asserted. Pride of place was given to Robert Boyle, whose bust was on a plinth higher than the others, his head set against a painted sunburst. Where the idea for the busts originated is not clear, but the bust of Newton was clearly anticipated by the painting of Newton's profile in Grantham.

The hermitage proved to be hugely popular, so Queen Caroline soon embarked on a related fantasy: a druidic Merlin's Cave. It had a Gothic arched entrance, timber and plaster walls, and a thatched roof in the shape of a beehive. This was the roof that inaugurated the fashion for thatched buildings in stately gardens. On 30 June 1735 the *Gentleman's Magazine* announced that this 'subterranean building' (actually a cave above ground) would be 'adorned with astronomical figures and characters'. On 21 August the same journal enumerated the six wax figures which the queen had ordered for the Cave: Merlin, Elizabeth of York (consort of Henry VII), Queen Elizabeth (coming to Merlin for knowledge), Minerva, Merlin's secretary (a boy), and a witch. All six figures were modelled from living people (for example, Merlin's secretary from a royal gardener, the witch from a Richmond tradesman's wife). These were the waxwork precursors of living ornamental hermits. This was a richly documented cave, partly because so many visitors wrote about the experience. Indeed, Edmund Curll wrote a 246-page book entitled *The rarities of Richmond: being exact descriptions of the Royal Hermitage and Merlin's Cave. With his life and prophecies*, of which the second edition (1736) is 'adorned with cuts' that include detailed images of the hermitage and the cave.

The Queen ordered that a selection of English books be placed in the Cave, and appointed Stephen Duck as 'cave and library keeper' and his wife Sarah Big as 'necessary woman'. Duck was an agricultural labourer who had become a court poet, but was still a 'natural man' in Rousseau's sense of the term, and so was an ideal custodian for the Cave. In a poem 'On Richmond Park and the Royal Gardens' Duck hymned the busts in the Hermitage:

> bear me, Nymphs, to the sequestered cell,
> Where BOYLE and NEWTON, mighty sages, dwell;
> Whose fame shall live, although the Grot decay,
> Long as those sacred truths their works display.

Not all poets took the same adulatory view. An anonymous contributor to the April 1733 issue of the *Gentleman's Magazine* (which contained several poems and essays on the subject of the hermitage) clearly disapproved, reserving special obloquy for Clarke's allegedly Arian ('unchristian') convictions:

> And here is built a clumsy heap,
> Thought beautiful in ruin.
> Three holes there are, through which you see,
> Three seats to set your a—e on;

> And idols four—of wizards three,
> And one unchristian parson.

In a loftier vein, Alexander Pope's 'Epistle to Lord Burlington' (Richard Boyle, earl of Burlington, from the same family as Robert Boyle) counselled 'nor in an hermitage set Dr Clarke'. Jonathan Swift published three of the many poems on the subject, and one of the three, called 'On the Hermitage at Richmond', he had written himself. In the first line, 'Lewis' is King Louis XIV, who in 1666 had founded the French Académie des Sciences.

> Lewis the living learned fed,
> And raised the scientific head:
> Our frugal Queen to save her meat,
> Exalts the heads that cannot eat.

As it happens, the 'Grot' never had a chance to decay, because both the Hermitage and Merlin's Cave were destroyed when Capability Brown remodelled the gardens in 1765. The five busts survived, and were identified at Windsor in 1922; they remain in the Royal Collection, and are now in the Privy Chamber at Kensington Palace.

The second English hermitage was also the work of William Kent, who in the early 1730s worked at Stowe (Buckinghamshire) as well as Richmond (and at Alexander Pope's house at Twickenham). Stowe was the seat of Richard Temple, first Viscount Cobham, a prominent politician and friend of Pope. One of the many remarkable features of Lord Cobham's garden at Stowe is that it was always open to visitors. Indeed, in 1717 he opened the New Inn on the edge of the grounds to accommodate them (it was long derelict but was restored and opened as a visitor centre in 2011), and he sponsored successive editions of a guidebook to the gardens. This was the first guidebook designed for use in an English garden.

One of Kent's earliest follies at Stowe was the hermitage (1731), which was a version of the hermitage for Queen Caroline at Richmond. The Stowe hermitage did not accommodate busts, but four years later Kent built the Temple of British Worthies (1735) at Stowe, and it displays an abundance of busts. The hermitage is a rough stone building with an arched opening and two towers, one of which was built as a ruin. The pediment over the door is decorated with a wreath and pan pipes. The interior is a square room with groin vaulting; seating consists of three stone benches set in niches. The building is surrounded by trees to enhance the sense of delightful gloom. As William Gilpin commented in 1748, the siting of the hermitage 'in the midst of this delightful wilderness, has an exceeding good effect: it is of the romantic kind; and beauties of this sort, where a probable nature is not exceeded, are generally pleasing'. The sense of pleasure can still be felt today: the trees are now mature, and the view across Eleven Acre Lake to Home Park is still delightful.

There was no hermit in residence at Stowe, but this vacancy was soon filled through the imagination of Gilbert West (nephew of Viscount Cobham), whose poem about Stowe gardens (1732) explained that the hermitage was the final residence of Malbecco, the aged, grumpy, miserly husband of the young, beautiful, and unfaithful Hellenore in Book III of Edmund Spenser's *Faerie Queene*. In Spenser's tale, Hellenore sets fire to Malbecco's treasury and then runs off with her lover Paridell and becomes the mistress of a group of satyrs. This story was represented in paintings in the Temple of Venus (constructed by Kent at the same time as the hermitage), and West

FIGURE 4.3 The hermitage, Stowe.

extended the narrative by accommodating the angry and aggrieved Malbecco in the nearby hermitage.

Kent's hermitages at Richmond and Stowe inaugurated the fashion for ornamental hermitages in landscape gardens. Their attraction, as John Perceval (first earl of Egmont) recorded in his diary with reference to Richmond, was that they were 'very solitary and romantic'. Such qualities do not, however, necessitate adherence to any particular architectural tradition. After Kent, the fashion shifted to an even more naturalistic style, that of the root house.

The English root house

The root house has traditionally been thought to be an innovation of the second quarter of the eighteenth century. The publication in 2000 of John Evelyn's *Elysium Britannicum* overturned that comfortable assumption. In an encyclopaedic chapter on 'rocks, grotts, crypts, mounts, precipices, porticos, ventiducts', Evelyn describes a building which he calls a 'dry grott', explaining with disconcerting vagueness that

> we once observed a dry grott artificially made with the extravagant & vast roots of trees, which had been grubbed up, congested and heaped upon one another.... These were fastened in many places with wires and iron work and it was so covered with natural ivy that...we never beheld a more delightful spectacle. This kind of dry grott...[is] most fit for retirement and holy solitude, to which a lamp hanging in the farthest and darkest part will contribute, as greatly disposing to devotion and profound contemplation: for so the holy hermits lived in the times of persecution.

This passage, which is a corrected draft (the word 'holy' is a significant later addition), is ambivalent about the spiritual dimension and wholly uninformative about time and place, but it is clear that what Evelyn is describing is what would later be called a root house, which was a type of hermitage constructed or decorated with gnarled roots. The *Elysium* is primarily a work of the 1650s, and this passage shows that at least one root house existed in the mid-seventeenth century.

The architectural antecedents of the hermitage in the form of a root house are not abundant, but one visual source seems to have had some impact: the hermitages drawn in the sixteenth century by Marten de Vos and engraved by Jan and Raphael Sadeler were widely known, and the designs of the hermitages are broadly similar to those of English root houses. It should be noted that not all root houses were designated as hermitages. In addition to Mayfield, there is a surviving Georgian root house at Bix Bottom, near Bix House (Oxfordshire), and The Leasowes had three root houses as well as a hermitage.

FIGURE **4.4** Jan Sadeler, 'Origen building a hermit's cell', in *Solitudo, sive vitae partum eremicolarum.*

The earliest surviving English example of a root house was built in 1747 at Badminton, the Gloucestershire estate of the dukes of Beaufort. This building, which is known as the Hermit's Cave, was designed by Thomas Wright, the astronomer and landscape gardener. Wright's judgements in astronomy were occasionally right (he seems, for example, to have been the first to argue that our galaxy is shaped like a disc) but usually wrong, and his candidacy for a fellowship of the Royal Society was unsuccessful. He made a living in a succession of country houses, serving as tutor in mathematics and astronomy for young ladies and as a garden designer in the 'natural' style of William Kent; in this latter capacity he designed at least fifteen gardens. He worked for a time at Badminton in the service of

Charles Noel Somerset, fourth duke of Beaufort. At Badminton Wright designed a hermitage which was built in a wood; the hermitage survives, but the woodland does not, so the building now stands exposed in the park rather than hidden amongst the trees. A drawing of the hermitage made in the 1750s by an artist called Thomas Robins was acquired for the nation in 2000 (in lieu of inheritance tax) and is now in the Victoria and Albert Museum.

The drawing shows several features which have since disappeared, including a small turret rising from the thatched roof, two rustic chairs which were normally placed in a niche at the rear of the building, and an inscription above the doorway. The inscription read 'Obscurum verborum ambage novorum | Urganda heic carmen magico demurmurat ore, English'ed "Here Urganda in woods dark and perplexed, inchantments mutters with her magic voice"'. An understanding of this inscription required knowledge

FIGURE 4.5 The hermitage, Badminton c.1910.

FIGURE 4.6 Thomas Robins, drawing of Badminton hermitage (watercolour and pencil on paper).

of literary works not now widely read, so I shall attempt an explanation. The English translation includes the phrase 'woods dark and perplexed', which does not occur in the Latin, but rather derives from the *selva oscura* ('dark wood') at the beginning of Dante's *Inferno* and the 'perplexed paths of this drear wood' in Milton's *Comus*. The Latin is an adaptation of Ovid's *Metamorphoses* (14.57–8) in which 'Urganda heic' ('here Urganda') is substituted for 'Ter noviens' ('thrice nine times'). The effect of the change was to substitute Urganda for Ovid's enchantress Circe. Urganda was a protector with magical powers who first appeared in the medieval Spanish and Portuguese romance *Amadís de Gaula* and had played a central role in Lord Lansdowne's musical tragedy called *The British Enchanters, or No Magic like Love* (1706), which had been a triumph at the new Haymarket Theatre. One of the preliminary verses to Lord Lansdowne's play explains why Urganda might be placed in a garden:

> Let sage Urganda wave the circling wand
> On barren mountains, or a waste of sand,
> The desert smiles, the woods begin to grow
> The birds to warble and the springs to flow.

Urganda has become the tutelary deity of Badminton, and her cave a suitable habitat for a hermit.

The rough exterior of the Badminton hermitage is set within a wooden frame of corner posts, pediments, and lintels. The walls are made of branches, roots, and chunks of wood. The thatched roof once supported a cross. At the rear of the building, the alcove which originally contained the chairs has been replaced by a bench with an inscription in which the letters are outlined with nailheads: 'Here loungers loiter, here the weary wait'. At the front of the building, the doorway with its pointed arch has been fashioned from the inverted fork of a tree. Above the doorway the ironwork of a roundel survives, but the stained glass does not. Inside, to the surprise of the visitor, there is a Palladian room, now dilapidated but nonetheless with sturdy architectural features, including pilasters and a ribbed vault (the plan of the room seems to be identical to the main room of the menagerie that Thomas Wright designed for Horton House, in Northamptonshire). The room is lit by two-light Gothic windows; the shutters have decorative patterns in bark. On the wooden floor there are telltale signs of the hand of Wright in the form of nailhead outlines of mathematical figures. A Greek inscription (*dos pou sto*) alludes to the boast of Archimedes with respect to his discovery of the mechanics of the lever: *dos pou sto kai ton kosmon kineso* (give me a place to stand and I will move the world). An alcove at the back has a flat wall, and so seems likely to have held a painting. The interior was once decorated with moss, which has all but gone. The only furniture that survives is a table fashioned from the bole of an elm; the rustic chairs that once surrounded it have disappeared. There is an undocumented tradition that a costumed servant worked as a part-time hermit. Alternatively, the mathematical figures may imply that Thomas Wright was a part-time hermit. In Tom Stoppard's *Arcadia*, for which Badminton may have provided a model, the mathematics tutor becomes the hermit.

The most influential root house of the eighteenth century was constructed at Stourhead (Wiltshire) in 1770. The garden, which is one of the most beautiful in England, was created by Henry Hoare, a scion of the banking family. Hoare's Bank was founded in 1672 and is now (as C. Hoare & Co.) the only surviving private deposit bank of the many that were established before the nineteenth century. Hoare inherited a splendid Palladian house at Stourhead, and when he moved into the house in 1741 he set about transforming the landscape. In 1744 he commissioned Henry Flitcroft to design appropriate classical buildings, all of which were set on high ground. The buildings were integrated features of the landscape, but also served as galleries in which Hoare's sculpture collection could be displayed. Flitcroft designed the Temple of Ceres (1744–6; now the Temple of Flora), the Temple of Hercules (1753–4; now the Pantheon), a grotto (1748; enlarged 1776), and the cave (1751). The small River Stour was dammed in 1754 to create the large lake that makes the garden so idyllic, and in 1765 Flitcroft added the Temple of Apollo. These buildings all survive, but the hermitage on which Hoare embarked in about 1770 does not. He described the project in a letter to his grand-daughter Harriet, explaining that he was

> building a hermitage. . . . It is to be lined inside and out with old gouty nobbly oaks, the bark on. [One of the oaks was] . . . called Judge Wyndham's Seat which I take to be of the Year of our Lord 1000, and I am not quite sure it is not antediluvian. I believe I shall put it in to be myself the Hermit.

Judge Wyndham's Oak, in the Dorset village of Silton (near Gillingham), is one of England's most famous trees; it is even marked on Ordnance Survey maps.

The seventeenth-century judge Sir Hugh Wyndham was said to have been so enamoured with the view from beneath the tree that he had a seat installed there. Hoare's comment may imply that it was fashioned from Judge Wyndham's Oak, in which case it was indeed ancient, though possibly not antediluvian.

When the valley was flooded to make the lake, Hoare commissioned a path around the lake that would link the garden buildings. On the advice of his friend Charles Hamilton (of Painshill), Hoare situated his hermitage on the path that led to the Temple of Apollo (now the rocky path on the far side of the road that runs alongside the gardens). Close to the temple, a tunnel was constructed over the path, so visitors to the temple first entered the tunnel through the hollow of a tree, and then turned into the hermit's cell, which was furnished with a chair and an altar made from the stump of a tree. The hermitage was dismantled in 1814, but its appearance is known both from written accounts and from a drawing done by the Swedish garden designer Fredrik Magnus Piper during a visit to England (see Plate 1). The tunnel was constructed from inverted oak trunks, with the upturned roots intertwined like a peristyle (in the architecture of

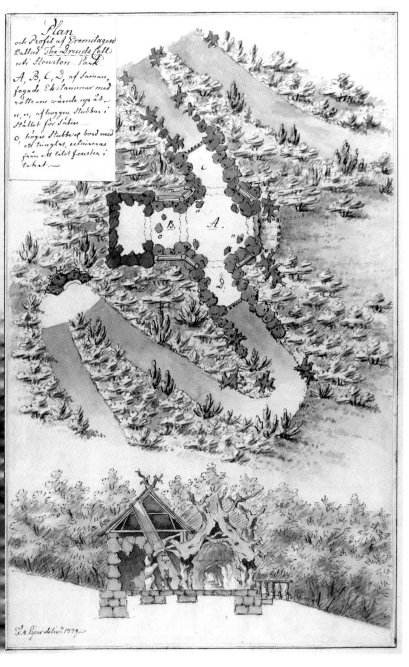

PLATE 1 F. M. Piper, drawing of the hermitage at Stourhead. The Swedish heading means 'Plan and Profile of the Hermitage called The Druid's Cell at Stourton Park [i.e. Stourhead]/ A, B, C, D, joined oak trunks with the roots turned upwards/ n, n, hewn stumps instead of seats/ a higher stump or table with an hourglass, lit by a small window in the roof'.

PLATE 2 The hermitage, Spetchley Park, Worcestershire.

PLATE 3 The hermitage, Brocklesby Park.

PLATE 4 Samuel Hieronymous Grimm, *The Hermitage at Selborne, Hampshire, with Henry White as the Hermit*, 1777.

PLATE 5 John Phillp, Interior of the hermitage at Soho.

PLATE 6 (*above*) The Bear's Hut,
Killerton.

PLATE 7 (*left*) The hermitage,
Eastbourne.

PLATE 8 The Hermitage at Oriel Temple

PLATE 9 The Hermitage, Tollymore.

PLATE 10 Dunkeld Hermitage.

PLATE 11 Geraint Evans, *An Ornamental Hermit* (2007).

PLATE 12 The hermit of Arlesheim.

classical antiquity, a peristyle is a range of columns surrounding a building). This rustic gesture towards an ancient architectural structure neatly combines the classical impulse with an insistence that the style be true to nature. This was also a hermitage with a view, in this case over one of England's finest man-made landscapes.

The hermitages at Richmond, Stowe, Badminton, and Stourhead are particularly well documented, but less is known about scores of others. In Chapter 3 I examined hermitages with hermits (Painshill, Hawkstone, Woodhouse, Tong, Selborne, Vauxhall Gardens) and hermitages for which hermits were sought (Atherton Hall, Barrow House). Now I shall turn to hermitages with imaginary inhabitants. The only imaginary hermit resident in London was Padre Giovanni. There is no evidence for hermitages in East Anglia, but other regions of England all had hermitages in the Georgian period, some of which survive. We shall consider the stories of hermitages and their builders in the Midlands, the North of England, the West Country, and the Home Counties. As the Midlands estates with hermitages form a more coherent group than is the case elsewhere, it seems sensible to begin there.

The Midlands

Several estates in the Midlands were linked by social networks, one of which had a literary manifestation in the circle known as the Warwickshire Coterie (William Shenstone, Richard Jago, and William Somervile). The muse of these poets was Henrietta Knight, Lady Luxborough (Viscount Bolingbroke's half-sister), who in 1736 had been banished to her husband's derelict Warwickshire estate of Barrells because of two adulterous affairs. The poets ignored this unhappy background, and praised her as the heavenly Asteria. The correspondence between Lady Luxborough and her poetical admirers often touched on landscape gardening, as did her wider correspondence with women friends around the country. In this respect she played a role similar to that of Mrs Delany in Ireland.

The most important of Lady Luxborough's poets was William Shenstone, who was born on his family's farm, called The Leasowes. The farm was on the edge of Halesowen, which was then an exclave of Shropshire, later assigned to Worcestershire and now in the metropolitan county of West Midlands. In 1744, aged 30, Shenstone moved back to his childhood home, and embarked on the transformation of the farm into a *ferme ornée* (ornamented farm), which is a working farm to which ornamental features have been added to create a 'natural' landscape. The *ferme ornée* was discussed more often than it was created, and The Leasowes is the only surviving example in England that is accessible to the public (in Ireland there is another fine (and recently restored) surviving example open to the public, Larchill Arcadian Garden, in County Kildare).

At The Leasowes Shenstone aspired to re-create the world of Virgil. His garden is a realization of Virgil's *Eclogues* (pastoral poems) and *Georgics* (poems about farming). Shenstone drove home the point by signposting many features in the garden with quotations from Virgil and by designating part of the garden as 'Virgil's Grove', where he erected an obelisk in honour of the poet. In the gardens Shenstone built a ruined priory, temples, seats, and a cottage. There were many urns and benches, often with inscribed quotations. Several of the larger features were designed by the architect Sanderson Miller.

The arrangement of the garden features reflected an aspiration to be natural, but nonetheless conformed to the ideal of structured and melancholic contemplation of picturesque landscape. Within this designed 'natural' landscape there were three root houses, one of which was dedicated to the fourth earl of Stamford, whose estate was at nearby Enville (see below), and a hermitage. The root houses contributed to the atmosphere that Shenstone sought to create. His friend the bookseller and writer Robert Dodsley, for example, describes with gusto how 'a gloomy walk leads to a root house in a sequestered corner'. The hermitage, which was built in 1740 (at the outset of Shenstone's building programme), took the form of an excavated cave surmounted by a cross, just below a Gothic alcove that was known as the hermit's seat. It was not a prominent building, but rather part of what was to become a larger architectural ensemble of a dozen buildings that collectively embodied Shenstone's ideal of melancholic contemplation.

Visitors to The Leasowes were welcome, and came in abundance, among them William Gilpin, Horace Walpole, and Thomas Whately. Guides to the garden were published by Robert Dodsley, and by Joseph Heely, a landowner from nearby Kings Norton who wrote *Letters on the Beauties of Hagley, Envil and The Leasowes with critical remarks and Observations on the Modern Taste in Gardening*. Thomas Jefferson recorded his visit in *Memorandums Made on a Tour to Some of the Gardens in England* (1786) and Lord Byron wrote 'Verses Found in a Summer-house at Halesowen' (*c.*1812). As Dr Johnson commented, Shenstone's transformation of The Leasowes was accomplished 'with such judgement and such fancy as made his little domain the envy of the great and the admiration of the skilful: a place to be visited by travellers, and copied by designers'. The

Leasowes has only been copied once, on a small scale at nearby Woodhouse, but it was certainly imitated, most notably at Ermenonville and at Thomas Jefferson's Monticello, and, in the late twentieth century, at Little Sparta, the garden of the poet Ian Hamilton Finlay at Stonypath, in Lanarkshire. The Leasowes is now undergoing restoration in a programme that may eventually include the re-creation of the hermitage.

Shenstone and his poetry enjoyed considerable standing in the eighteenth century, but there were sceptics, one of whom was Shenstone's friend Richard Graves, who wrote a satirical novel entitled *Columella, or, The Distressed Anchoret, a colloquial tale* (1779). The eponymous hero of *Columella*, who gained a niche in immortality when he was mentioned by Mrs Dashwood in *Sense and Sensibility*, is modelled loosely on Shenstone. Columella is described as 'an incurable melancholic', and his melancholia is attributed to the idle solitude of rural retirement. In the course of the novel an old man applies to be Columella's hermit, with a view to sitting in the door of the hermitage with a book whenever visitors passed by. He is dismissed on the grounds that Columella is 'an hermit himself, and lived in his own wood'.

Shenstone's circle of friends included his horticultural rival Sir George Lyttelton (later first Baron Lyttelton and secretary to Frederick Lewis, Prince of Wales), who aspired to shape Hagley Park (Worcestershire) into a landscape garden that would surpass the accomplishments of Shenstone at The Leasowes and his uncle Richard Temple, the first Viscount Cobham, at Stowe. Lyttelton worked from 1747 to 1764 to enhance the spectacular landscape that he inherited. The outstanding garden that he created (with the advice of the landscape architect Charles Hamilton) has in substantial part survived to the present day, thanks to the conservationist impulses of the Cobham family (the twelfth Viscount Cobham is now the custodian of Hagley). George Lyttelton wanted buildings in his landscape, and friends such as Thomas Pitt (first Baron Camelford), Henry Keene, Thomas Pitt of Encombe House (Isle of Purbeck, Dorset), James 'Athenian' Stuart, and (most important of all) Sanderson Miller contributed designs for these follies, which include a hermitage, an obelisk, an Ionic rotunda, a Palladian bridge, a 'ruined' quasi-medieval tower, and a set of four stones known as 'Ossian's Tomb'. This 'tomb' of a non-existent bard, on the summit of Clent Hill, became the best known of the follies. In 1753 Horace Walpole, whose judgements were often austere, declared that 'I wore out my eyes with gazing, my feet with climbing, and my tongue and vocabulary with commending'.

The features of Hagley included a set of four rustic buildings in a copse known as Hermitage Wood. The precise date of their construction is not known, but if they were as early as 1739, then some of the buildings may have been constructed to the designs of Alexander Pope, who is known to have designed three (unspecified) buildings for Hagley. The four structures, in the order in which visitors were intended to see them, were a seat of contemplation, a hermitage, a root house, and a pebble alcove. The seat of contemplation was a curved bench sheltered by an alcove decorated with sheep bones and shells. An inscription laid out in snail shells named the seat in Latin (*Sedes Contemplationis*), and added the biblical phrase *omnia vanitas*, the Vulgate version of Ecclesiastes 1:2, translated in the King James Bible as 'all is vanity'. The root house, which was built against a bank and roofed with turf, was made of tree stumps and furnished with a chair made of sticks. The pebble alcove, which Heely calls 'a sort of cell', was decorated with patterned pebbles.

The hermitage was a square building made from stumps, roots, and tree trunks in which the gaps were filled with earth and moss. Inside there were two rooms with pebbled floors. A drawing of the hermitage made by the politician Sir John Parnell in 1769 (preserved in the library of the LSE) includes a plan that shows only one room, so the internal partition seems at some point to have been removed. On seeing the hermitage, 'on the brow of a shady mountain, stealing peeps into the glorious world below', Walpole declared it to be 'exactly like those in Sadeler's prints' (see p. 109). The fullest account is that of Joseph Heely, who took careful note both of the setting of the hermitage and of the ideals that shaped it:

> This place is formed with clumps of wood, and jagged roots of old trees, carelessly thrown together, and the interstices are simply filled up with various kinds of moss; the floor is neatly paved with small pebbles, and a sort of couch goes round, covered with a mat. Everything about it carries the face of poverty, and a contempt of the vain superfluities of life, fit for the supposed inhabitant, who despises the follies of the world, and devotes his hours to religious solitude.
>
> Not a recess in the whole park is more to be desired than this; the constant melody of birds, perching unseen, within the rich foliage of the finest groves in the world—the boldness of the ground, the deep-formed vales, whose embellished sides, and sometimes bottoms, of chestnuts, elms and oaks, rise gracefully to the sight; together with the calm, undisturbed repose which hovers round it, throws the mind into a contemplation, equally serious and affecting. Within the hermitage are those celebrated lines from the 'Il Penseroso' of Milton:
>
> > And may at last my weary age
> > Find out the peaceful hermitage,
> > The hairy gown and mossy cell
> >
> > . . . .

> There appear from the door of this mossy apartment two views in perspective agreeably blended with the closeness of the others: one very prettily catches a range of country *over* the spreading boughs of the fronting trees, and the other *under* them. Little fancies of this sort, in places so solitary, where they do not expose the situation, but only tincture the surrounding gloom with a ray of cheerfulness, are very justificable.

This lyrical description underlines the ideal of melancholy. In Heely's view, a hint of cheerfulness is as much as can be allowed in an ornamental hermitage, because the ambient feeling must be gloomy.

And who was the hermit of Hagley? Heely explains in one of his *Letters* that

> Everything within and immediately about it [carried] the face of poverty and a contempt for the vain superfluity of the world, fit out for the imaginary inhabitant, whom we are led to suppose despises the follies and luxuries of life, and who devoted his melancholy hours to meditation and a rigid abstinence.

The hermit is one of a long line of imaginary hermits, present only in the minds of those who visited the Hagley hermitage.

At least one visitor seems to have taken a more cynical view. Joseph Giles (an occasional poet of whom nothing is known apart from his acquaintance with Shenstone and his residence in Birmingham) composed 'A Parody upon those Lines of Milton's in the Hermitage at Hagley Park':

> May I, while health and strength remains,
> And blood flows warm within my veins;
> Find out some virgin, soft and kind,
> Who is to social joy inclined;
> A nymph who can for me forgo,
> The fop, the fribble, and the beau;
> From noise and show, content can be,
> To live at home with love and me:

> Such pleasures Love and Hymen give,
> And such a life I wish to live.

These lines are a salutary reminder that not everyone subscribed to the ideology of the hermit and his hermitage.

Another estate in the vicinity was Enville Hall, which was the Stafford-shire seat of the earls of Stamford for centuries, and is still occupied by members of the family. Between 1745 and 1755 Harry Grey, the fourth earl, created a landscape garden of some 750 acres (300 hectares), and both Shenstone and Sanderson Miller contributed to the design. In the late 1940s a decaying bark-clad hermitage was photographed for a book by Osvald Sirén, but in the informed view of Sandy Haynes, the archivist of Enville, the building in Sirén's photograph was not a hermitage but rather a summer house on the edge of the lawn. Similarly, there is no reference to a hermitage in the estate records. It is possible that an Enville hermitage escaped the documentary record, but also possible such a building never existed. There is a ruined cottage on the estate that was described in 1756 as a 'pheasantry and hermitage for the keeper of the fowl', but its human occupants were all women tasked with looking after the fowl, and were not required to act the part of a hermit.

These estates all had links with Barrells, Lady Luxborough's estate, and with Woodhouse, which was discussed in the previous chapter. At Barrells Lady Luxborough constructed a *ferme ornée* (and in describing her garden coined the term 'shrubbery'). On one occasion she told her neighbour William Shenstone that

> a Mr Gough of Perry-Hall was here, about three weeks ago, to ask leave to see my hermitage, and said he liked it. I do not enjoy it much

myself: the cold weather and incessant rain would hinder me, were I even in better spirits. Indeed you will say, it is just a proper place for indulging melancholy thoughts, which is true, but therefore I ought to shun it.

It seems that Lady Luxborough had reservations about the desirability of the melancholy induced by her hermitage.

There is another reference to the Barrells hermitage in a letter from Shenstone to Lady Luxborough in which he declares that he is 'glad to hear of every contrivance near your Hermitage that seems likely to tend to the Hermitess's repose'. There is no hint of what these contrivances might be, nor is the identity of the hermitess elucidated: it is remotely possible that this is the only instance of a female ornamental hermit, but much more likely that Lady Luxborough is fashioning herself as a hermitess. No record survives of the physical appearance of Lady Luxborough's hermitage, nor is it clear whether Mr Gough built one at Perry Hall; his house was demolished in 1927, and only the moat remains.

In 1761, close to Perry Hall, in what is now another suburb of Birmingham, the manufacturer and entrepreneur Matthew Boulton decided to supplement his Birmingham factory at Snow Hill with another on Handsworth Heath. The cottage on the heath was rebuilt as Soho House, and the rolling mill in the valley below was demolished to make way for a new factory and accommodation for his workers. Soho House became Boulton's home, and it was there that he entertained fellow members of the Lunar Society of Birmingham (including James Watt, Erasmus Darwin, Josiah Wedgwood, and Joseph Priestley), a group of prominent Midlands intellectuals and inventors. The house was rebuilt in the 1790s, and it was in this period that a hermitage was erected in the garden. The remodelling of the house was initially undertaken by James Wyatt, but when he began to drift away from the project it was finished by his brother Samuel. The architecture of James Wyatt had a Gothic dimension, but Samuel Wyatt's buildings were resolutely neoclassical, so if one of the brothers designed the hermitage, it was probably James. Boulton's own design interests ranged from steam engines to buttons, so it is also possible that he designed it himself, but there are two additional possibilities: in 1795 Boulton paid the architect William Hollins to give lessons in architectural drawings to John Phillp, who may have been Boulton's natural son, and either Hollins or Phillp could be responsible for the hermitage, which Boulton described as his 'building adapted for contemplation'.

Three images by Phillp depict the hermitage when it was new. A pen and ink drawing of 1795 shows a circular building with two Gothic latticed windows that appear to be glazed; the exterior is faced with bark and the pointed roof is thatched with ling (heather). An undated companion image in which watercolour is added to pen-and-ink shows the hermitage covered in snow. A watercolour painted in 1799 shows part of the interior (see Plate 5). This painting depicts a pointed Gothic door with glass panelling and two windows covered with translucent cloth swags of a sort sometimes used for mourning. A plaque between the door and the first window has at the top 'A faithful record of the virtues of', but the rest is blank, awaiting the name of the departed. Between the two windows there is an oval image of a man (possibly masked) in profile. Objects hanging on the surround include a lamp and a pair of boots. In short, the decoration is designed to facilitate melancholic contemplation.

In 1995 Soho House became a museum that honours Matthew Boulton and the Lunar Society. The garden has now been restored with reference to Matthew Boulton's original planting lists, and reconstructions include the hermitage, which is closer to the house than the original, but otherwise replicates it in every known detail.

Spetchley Park, a few miles east of Worcester, has been the home of the Berkeley family since 1605. In 1804 Robert Berkeley inherited Spetchley Park from his uncle (the Robert Berkeley who wrote a well-known life of Cardinal Pole), and built a new house in the Palladian style (finished in 1811). Shortly thereafter he commissioned the construction of a root house for the garden. The design was adapted from an arbour illustrated on the frontispiece of the first volume of Thomas Wright's *Universal Architecture* (1755). The frame of the hermitage consists of eight elm pillars (see Plate 2). The front three bays are open, and the other five are filled in with hazel coppice arranged in geometrical patterns. Two of the walls have ogee windows which probably contained coloured glass. The thatched roof is pyramidical, and has a central boss of elm. The pebbled floor may once have been patterned. There is a hazel bench fitted to the interior wall. The fact that the front bays are open implies that the building did not have a resident hermit, and may rather have served as a garden pavilion.

Derbyshire has many fine stately homes, one of which is Kedleston Hall. In 1758 Nathaniel Curzon, first Lord Scarsdale, inherited the estate and immediately ordered that the existing Queen Anne house be demolished to clear the way for a Palladian mansion to be designed by Robert Adam. Adam's brief extended to the buildings in the gardens, and it is likely that the hermitage was one of his designs. The plan for the hermitage depicts a thatched circular building surrounded by a peristyle of eleven columns; the single room (which in the plan has no windows) had a diameter of five metres. The hermitage was erected in 1761–2 in the Long Walk, half a mile west of the south front of the house. The Long Walk had been laid out in 1760 and planted with trees and shrubs. The path is now flanked with mature trees, and the hermitage is in heavy shade. It is clear that the building does not correspond precisely to the plan. What survives is a red brick building (coursed with rubble) with a diameter of about two metres; the interior is lined with brick. There is a round-arched doorway, and two square window openings. It was re-thatched in 1860, but is now an overgrown ruin encased in corrugated iron. A nearby sign proclaims the intention of the National Trust to restore the hermitage when funds permit; it would be a splendid project.

Elsewhere in Derbyshire, three medieval rock hermitages which had once accommodated pious troglodyte inhabitants were restored as recreational venues for gentry families on whose land they lay. First, at Cratcliffe Cave near Birchover, a real hermit's cave (with medieval stone carvings) was 'improved' in the eighteenth century by the local vicar, who also built viewing terraces and carved stone armchairs in the vicinity of the hermitage, which is on the face of the cliff. I could not find the armchairs, but can assure the reader that the carved Crucifixion in the cave is worth a detour. Second, Sir Robert Burdett, who was the proprietor of the splendid Palladian Foremarke Hall (now Repton Preparatory School), adapted the nearby 'Anchor Church' at Foremark (which is spelt without the final 'e') for parties; a painting of 1762 by Thomas Smith of Derby (now in the Derby Museum and Art Gallery) shows a family picnic at the cave. The name 'anchor' is not maritime, but rather refers to the tradition that an anchorite was incarcerated in the cave before the Reformation. Third, at Dale Abbey, which until the Reformation had been occupied by Præmonstratensian Canons ('White Canons'), there was a hermitage carved into a cliff on the edge of the monastic complex. The hermit eventually moved down the hill to more comfortable accommodation, and the hermitage was abandoned until it was adapted for social purposes by the Stanhope family in the eighteenth century.

There are also medieval rock hermitages in Worcestershire (Southstone Rock, Stourport-on-Severn, Wolverley) and Shropshire (Bridgnorth) that may have been adapted for family use in the eighteenth century, but in many cases evidence is wanting. The façade of the Redstone Rock caves at Stourport, for example, seems too architectural to be natural, but no documentation supports that judgement. At Downton Castle (Herefordshire), however, the connoisseur

FIGURE 4.7 'Anchor Church' at Foremark, Derbyshire.

FIGURE 4.8 The hermitage, Dale Abbey.

and collector Richard Payne Knight remodelled a cave to serve as a rock hermitage suitable for entertaining.

The final Midlands hermitage of which note must be taken is Burley-on-the-Hill, in Rutland. There is a connection with Frogmore, because Princess Elizabeth's governess was Charlotte, countess of Winchilsea. Lady Charlotte was the daughter of the first earl of Pomfret and the wife of George Finch-Hatton, ninth earl of Winchilsea and fourth earl of Nottingham (and founder of the MCC, the Marylebone Cricket Club), whose seat from his Nottingham inheritance was at Burley-on-the-Hill, in Rutland. In 1807 the earl and countess built the hermitage known as the Sanctuary of the Hermit Finch, which was hidden in the trees behind the house. The hermitage was a circular building some six metres in diameter, constructed from chunks of wood (including its bark) and roofed with thatch. The window openings were neither glazed nor shuttered, but instead were fitted with open gratings, as was the doorway. Inside there was a sitting-room with a small bedroom at the back. Bosses of elm that had been distorted by a fungal disease decorated both exterior and interior. The fan-vaulted ceiling was infilled with bark. The floor was a mosaic made of pebbles and bones set in geometrical patterns with the initial 'W' (for 'Winchilsea') and the date 1807. Furnishings consisted of a table fashioned from diseased elm, with decorative bones on top, and four rustic chairs. A hanging made of twigs separated this room from the hermit's bedroom, which contained a rack bed covered with sacking. At the foot of the bed a stool was set into the wall for the benefit of supplicants who might wish to visit the hermit while he reclined in bed. The hermitage contained two fireplaces, and this may be a sign that there was a hermit in residence, but it is equally possible that, as in so many ornamental hermitages, the hermit had just slipped out for a moment. In 1965 the hermitage was destroyed by a fire set by three local schoolboys.

FIGURE 4.9 The Sanctuary of the Hermit Finch, Burley-on-the-Hill.

North of England

The most remarkable surviving hermitage in the north of England is the root house at Brocklesby Park, the Lincolnshire seat of the Pelham family, who since 1837 have been the earls of Yarborough. In the 1780s Charles Anderson Pelham (later Baron Yarborough) commissioned Capability Brown to lay out the gardens and the architect Thomas Wyatt to construct suitable buildings for Brown's landscape, notably a fine mausoleum of 1786. As Wyatt and Brown did not include hermitages in their gardens, the root house on the estate may be a survivor from an earlier garden, possibly built in the 1760s; nothing is known of the circumstances of its construction. It is a small octagonal building in a wood at a considerable distance from the house, close to a tunnel grotto from which it was probably approached. The hermitage is constructed of brick and rock, and now has a slate roof, though it seems likely that it originally had a thatched roof and that the brick at the rear is a later addition. The entrance is a Gothic arch formed of curved tree trunks (see Plate 3). The walls are roughly laid rock supported by a frame of tree trunks. Inside, the ribbed pyramidical ceiling has bark bosses. The walls were surfaced with bark and patterned branches, of which some remain. Remarkably, what seems to be the original furniture survives inside, though it has been disfigured by vandals. There is a table made from a bole, a rustic hermit's chair formed from branches, and four chairs for visitors carved out of solid tree trunks. It is said that the hermitage once had a resident hermit, but no documentary evidence supports this tradition. It is a small building, and better suited to a visiting hermit who could appear whenever visitors approached the hermitage. This hermitage is a rare survivor, and is not in a good state of preservation, as the timber is deteriorating and there is no door. The Yarborough estate has carried out some splendid restorations of nearby temples, and it is to be hoped that, when funds permit, the Brocklesby hermitage will also be restored and secured.

There are three other hermitages to be noted in the north of England, all in Yorkshire. Little is known about a stone hermitage in Rawdon (a village now absorbed into Leeds) which survived into the twentieth century; it was an octagonal building with three open arches, and may have functioned as a gazebo in a garden that is now lost. Elsewhere in Leeds, Roundhay Park, which comprises more than 700 acres (280 hectares) of parkland, lakes, and woodland, was part of an ancient estate which belonged to the crown from the reigns of Henry IV to Henry VIII, and then passed through the Darcy family to the Barons Stourton. In 1803 the estate was divided into two portions. The northern part, which is now Roundhay Park, was sold

FIGURE 4.10 Interior of the hermitage, Brocklesby Park.

to Thomas Nicholson. This part of the estate had been mined and quarried, and the new owner transformed these eyesores into two lakes (the Upper Lake and the Waterloo Lake). In 1811 Nicholson embarked on a building programme which included a mansion house, a mock castle, and a hermitage. The appearance of the hermitage was recorded in photographs taken before World War I, after which it disappeared. The third Yorkshire hermitage was carved out of a boulder close to Falling Foss, a waterfall in the Esk Valley, near Whitby. The cave, which is declared by a carved inscription to be 'The Hermitage', is said to have been commissioned by George Chubb, the schoolmaster in nearby Littlebeck. His initials and the date 1790 are carved on the outside. Inside there is a bench intended to seat visitors to the waterfall, which can be heard while sitting in the cave. Additional seating is provided in two carved stone chairs on top of the boulder.

FIGURE 4.11 The hermitage, Roundhay Park, Leeds.

The West Country

The greatest concentration of hermitages in the West Country is in Devon. Oldstone, in Blackawton, was the seat of the Cholwich family from 1610 until 1800. The house remained unoccupied for several decades, after which it was the home of the Dimes family until the Palladian house was destroyed by fire in 1895. The Cholwiches seem to have developed the pleasure garden in the 1780s, building a sham fort, a shell-house, a grotto, and a slate rubble hermitage which consisted of a small vaulted cell; a recess at the back may have been a fireplace. The hermitage was reached by a path that passed through a stone archway on the edge of a wood. The archway had a plaque on which the opening verses of Thomas Parnell's 'The Hermit' were inscribed:

> Within a wild, unknown to public view
> From youth to age a reverend hermit grew

FIGURE 4.12 The hermitage, Oldstone.

> The moss his bed, the cave his humble cell,
> His food the fruits, his drink the crystal well,
> Remote from man, with God he passed the days
> Prayer all his business, all his pleasure praise.

It is possible that the Cholwiches had managed to engage such a low-maintenance hermit, but it seems more likely that this paragon of eremetical virtue was imaginary.

The Oldstone estate has now been absorbed into Woodlands Family Theme Park, in which the tradition of building follies has been continued with the construction of abbey ruins. The hermitage has survived in a quiet corner of the park, and is called the Monk's Cave; it now overlooks a pond ('Monk's Pool') with pedal boats. There is no sign of the plaque with Parnell's poem.

In 1761 the antiquary and topographer John Tripe inherited Oxton House, an estate near Exeter. In 1780 he changed his surname to Swete in order to inherit a substantial sum from a cousin. Swete spent some 40 years developing the gardens. His neighbour and fellow topographer Richard Polwhele declared that the grounds at Oxton 'are laid out in a style that perfectly accords with the modern fashion in gardening—since it is founded on the principles of NATURE and TRUTH'. In 1792 Swete erected a thatched Gothic hermitage, of which an image survives in an engraving (based on a drawing by Swete) in the series collectively known as *Beauties of England and Wales* (1801–16); there appears to be a hermit with a staff standing beside his hermitage. The estate has been broken up and is in divided private ownership. Many of the original features have been lost (the estate is now on English Heritage's 'At Risk' register), and there is no sign of the hermitage.

FIGURE **4.13** Engraving of Oxton, with a view of the hermitage.

The hermitage at Killerton, the Devonshire home of the Acland family, is known as the Bear's Hut (see Plate 6). The present house was built in the 1770s by Sir Thomas Dyke Acland, the ninth baronet, and the gardens were laid out by John Veitch, the first prominent member of a dynasty of horticulturalists; his descendants cared for the gardens until 1939. The hermitage, which was built in 1808, was a wedding gift from the politician and philanthropist Sir Thomas Acland, the tenth baronet, to his bride Lydia. The gift was a surprise, and was presented to Lady Acland when they returned from their honeymoon. Lady Acland was a member of the Hoare banking family, and thus related to the Hoares of Stourhead, so she was not the first member of her family to have a hermitage.

The Bear's Hut acquired its present name in the 1860s, when it accommodated a pet black bear brought from Canada by Gilbert Acland (grandson of Sir Thomas). It is arguably the finest hermitage in England, and it has been maintained in line with the uncompromising standards of the National Trust. Unless the bear was exceptionally well-behaved, the interior must have been restored at some point in the building's history, but the restoration is exemplary. The hermitage is constructed from rough wood arranged in patterns, and is thatched with wheat reed. The interior is divided into three rooms. The front opens into an entrance room with a cobbled floor and a ceiling fashioned from basket-weave wicker. Turning left, the visitor enters a central room with a floor inlaid with oak tree-trunk sections and a ceiling lined with matting and decorated with pine cones. The third room, into which the visitor peers over a half-door, is a hermit's chapel with a floor made of deer knucklebones (a variation on the usual choice of sheep knucklebones) and a ceiling of deer skins. This extraordinary chapel has rustic wooden versions of a chancel arch, a vaulted apse, and sedilia. The 'east window' of the chapel is a full-length lancet window inserted into a shaped tree trunk and fitted with Netherlandish painted glass panels, one of which is dated 1696.

Devon also contains a purpose-built rock hermitage. At Slade House in Salcombe Regis (a tiny village near Sidmouth), on the wooded side of a valley leading down to the sea, a circular hermit's cell with a large Gothic window and a doorway (surmounted by a small window) is set into the hillside. Much of the building is carved out of the rock. It has a cobbled floor, but the roof has gone. The building was commissioned in 1824 by a Mrs Leigh, apparently to accommodate a poet who planned to write an epic there. The hermitage is now cared for by the Donkey Sanctuary, which has laid out a series of well-maintained walks, one of which leads to the Hermitage.

FIGURE 4.14 The hermitage, Salcombe Regis.

The grandest of all English follies was Fonthill Abbey, in Wiltshire. Fonthill was the creation of William Thomas Beckford, the wealthiest commoner in England. The first stage of Fonthill Abbey was the construction of a mock convent, starting in 1796. Thereafter Beckford's megalomaniacal vision and deep pocket ensured that the building grew steadily until 1823, when the money finally ran out. The outbuildings included a hermitage on the west shore of the lake, now in ruins submerged in ivy. The building was a circular structure made from rustic tufa limestone, and the inner chambers resemble tunnels, but it is difficult to make inferences from what survives.

Fonthill Abbey was vast. At the other extreme, Lilliput Castle, a gentleman's villa near Bath, was tiny. It was built in 1738 by Jeremiah Peirce, a surgeon at the Mineral Water Hospital (now the Royal National Hospital for Rheumatic Diseases) and an intellectual and patron of the arts in the Enlightenment tradition. Peirce's eminent patients included Alexander Pope (who visited the villa) and Lady Luxborough, with whom he shared an informed interest in gardens. Lilliput Castle, which was designed by the visionary architect John Wood the elder (whose floor plan survives in Bath Central Library) was three storeys high (with the cellar floor largely sunk into the ground) but only six metres square. The ancient earthworks in the grounds of the villa include Bronze Age round barrows, an Iron Age dyke and what seems to be a Neolithic long barrow. Wood (and probably Peirce) understood these features to be the remains of an ancient druid settlement. The buildings that Peirce erected included a thatched hermitage (possibly designed by Wood), which is wholly consistent with the druidic environment. A book of sketchbook drawings by Thomas Robins the elder (now in the Victoria and Albert Museum) contains three pen-and-wash images of this hermitage. Visible details include a bell tower, a seat carved from a single tree trunk, and a human skull on the shelf just inside the door. On one of the three sketches, Robins has inscribed the usual lines from Milton's 'Il Penseroso'. After Peirce's death in 1765, Lilliput Castle was enlarged, and eventually grew into a Regency mansion called Battlefields; it has now been converted into flats, but Peirce's original building can still be discerned, because it forms the entrance hall. In 2006 the site of the hermitage (identified by the remains of the Gothic window) was discovered in the grounds (now Lilliput Farm) at the end of the paved yew and holly walk.

John Boyle, the fifth earl of Orrery, will feature in the next chapter because of his Irish hermitage, which is well known because of his published correspondence with his wife. What is less well known is that Lord Orrery also had an English estate, Marston House

FIGURE **4.15** Thomas Robins, the hermitage, Lilliput Castle.

(Somerset), and that there he constructed another hermitage. His friend Richard Pococke described it in July 1754:

> At the other end of the garden in a corner is a little hermitage near finished for my Lord's youngest son; there is a deep way down to it with wood on each side, a seat or two in it—one is made in the hollow of a tree; it leads to a little irregular court, with a fence of horses' heads and bones. It is a cabin, poorly thatched, and a bedstead covered with straw at one end, a chimney at the other, and some beginning made of very poor furniture.

'My Lord's youngest son' must be Edmund, born 21 November 1742. In July 1754 he would have been eleven, which seems an improbable age for melancholic contemplation.

There are occasional rediscoveries of lost hermitages, of which the best known is one found by Isabel Colegate. As she explains in her book on 'hermits, solitaries and wildernesses', she had read in a guidebook of 1791 that on land that she had recently acquired near her home at Midford Castle (Somerset),

> under a thick mass of shade, stands a rustic hermitage on the brow of the steep descent. The whole surrounding scenery is highly picturesque and romantic.

Midford Castle was built in 1775 for Henry Disney Roebuck from designs by draughtsman and antiquary John Carter; both men were Gothic enthusiasts, so it seems likely that the hermitage was designed by Carter. Isabel Colegate and her husband Michael Briggs rediscovered the ruins of the hermitage, and had it painstakingly reassembled; there was no sign of the roof, so they sensibly added a new one to secure the building. In the context of so many crumbling Georgian hermitages, the resurrection of a hermitage is good news.

The Home Counties

I shall survey hermitages in the Home Counties in a clockwise circle around London, beginning with the Royal County of Berkshire. The reason for the 'royal' designation of Berkshire is the presence of Windsor Castle and its Home Park. One of the estates within the Park is Frogmore. This chapter began with an account of the first royal hermitage in England, which was Queen Caroline's in Richmond Park. The second royal hermitage, sixty years later, was Queen Charlotte's, at Frogmore. In 1790 Little Frogmore was leased by King George III for Queen Charlotte; the adjoining Great Frogmore was acquired two years later, and the two gardens were amalgamated. The architect James Wyatt was commissioned to transform the enlarged estate into a retreat for the Queen and her daughters, following the precedent set by the Petit Trianon at Versailles. The Queen had a passionate and well-informed interest in horticulture and garden design, and promptly set about creating a 35-acre (14-hectare) landscaped garden with streams and a lake. By 1792 she had planted some 4,000 trees and shrubs in the Little Frogmore gardens, arranged to create a picturesque landscape. The acquisition of Great Frogmore occasioned the extension and redesign of the consolidated garden. The Queen's daughter Princess Elizabeth commissioned follies for the garden, collaborating with Wyatt on a Gothic ruin and implementing her own designs for an octagonal Temple of Solitude, a garden ballroom, and a hermitage. The hermitage was a circular building with a thatched roof and a thatched porch. As Mrs Delany, who introduced the garden hermitage to Ireland, was an intimate of the royal family, and had spent her final years living in a grace-and-favour house at Windsor (where she died in 1788), it is possible that this hermitage was the last manifestation of her role as the champion of such buildings.

In the early twentieth century the Frogmore garden was restored by Queen Mary, and in the late twentieth century again restored, this time to mark the silver jubilee of HM the Queen. The thatched hermitage has disappeared, as have the ballroom and the Temple of Solitude, but the Gothic ruin has survived, and has been ably restored. This building, which was used as a morning-room and tea house by Queen Victoria (before she commissioned the Tea House in 1869) seems to have been known in the early nineteenth century as the

Queen's Hermitage, and is labelled as such in an engraving of 1819. Another surviving building, known as the Swiss Seat, also has some characteristics of a garden hermitage, in that it is a brick hut faced with bark and gnarled bosses arranged as Gothic blind tracery. This building was erected close to the lake in 1833, and that date means that it must have been commissioned by Princess Augusta, who had been given the estate. There was no *hameau* at Frogmore, but there were many small garden buildings into which the women of the royal family could retreat.

In 1746 King George II appointed his third son (Prince William Augustus, duke of Cumberland) as ranger of Windsor Great Park. In the ensuing decades the duke employed large numbers of demobilized soldiers to create the lake now known as Virginia Water. From 1764 his deputy ranger was Thomas Sandby. In 1768 a dam made by Sandby burst, and he was thereafter mocked as 'Tommy Sandbank'. After another episode of serious flooding in 1782, Sandby formulated plans to make the lake more stable and more picturesque. Many of his drawings survive in the royal collection, including a design for a Gothic hermitage. Some of his plans for garden buildings were realized, including a grotto, but there is no evidence that the hermitage was ever built.

The correspondents of Lady Luxborough included Frances Seymour, countess of Hertford and later duchess of Somerset, who in 1739 acquired Riskins (now Richings Park), near Colnbrook, in Buckinghamshire. Riskins had been the estate of Earl Bathurst, who had created a landscape garden with a *ferme ornée*. Alexander Pope, who had been a guest at the house, complimented the garden in a couplet that mentions both Lord Bathurst and the earl of Burlington:

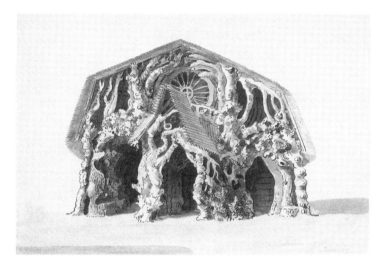

FIGURE 4.16 Thomas Sandby, design for a Gothic hermitage at Virginia Water.

> Who then shall grace, or who improve the soil,
> Who plants like Bathurst, or who builds like Boyle?

Lady Hertford renamed the estate Percy Lodge, and added to the garden a stone hexagon, an Indian 'bungola' (bungalow), and a hermitage. The estate and its châtelaine were much celebrated in country house poems that emphasized the contemplative life of Lady Hertford, and the hermitage is one of the features praised by the poets. The longest tribute is that of Moses Browne, of which these are the opening lines:

> Far in, a lonely cell is found
> On a small op'ning plat of ground,
> 'Twixt two tall elms that, tempest-proof,
> Rise stately o'er the craggy roof:
> And a torn arch above its height,
> Shews rudely-graceful to the sight.

143

> While up its buttress'd stone-cleft sides
> His foot a clamb'ring ivy guides,
> And hollies pale, and dark'ning yew
> The entrance keep with solemn view.

Many lines later, the poet declares that he would happily dwell as a hermit in this 'charming cell'.

On 31 December 1751 Lady Somerset, by now the dowager duchess, wrote to Lady Luxborough:

> As for the wise and witty of the present age…they will scarcely visit my hermitage; and I shall not leave it to visit them. I hope to dispose of my house in Downing Street; which I would not do if I ever intended to spend six weeks in London.

The passage is slightly puzzling, because it is not clear whether Lady Somerset is literally referring to her hermitage or describing Percy Lodge as a hermitage. In the event she retained both Percy Lodge and the house on Downing Street (No. 14, now demolished) until her death in 1754; Percy Lodge was destroyed by fire in 1786, and there is no trace of the hermitage.

Wrest Park, in Bedfordshire, was the seat of the de Grey family from the thirteenth century until 1917. In 1740 the estate passed to Jemima Yorke, Marchioness Grey, and three years later she moved with her husband (Philip Yorke, second earl of Hardwicke) to Wrest. Together they worked on the enhancement of the garden, and in August 1749 they erected a root house hermitage there. As this part of the garden had a druid theme (it was called the 'Mithraic Glade'), the hermitage was said to be the home of a priest of Mithras, and so was architecturally linked to the nearby 'Persian Altar'; both buildings were probably designed by Thomas Wright, who had been employed as a tutor in the house. The original house, which had been the subject of a poem by Thomas Carew, was demolished in the 1830s, but the early eighteenth-century garden was preserved. By the late twentieth century Wrest Park was derelict, but in 2006 English Heritage embarked on a 20 year project to restore the garden (and the present house), which opened to the public in 2011. The Persian Altar survives, but the humble hermitage is inevitably at the back of the queue for restoration.

The antiquarian Thomas Walford, who is best known as the author of *The Scientific Tourist through England, Wales, and Scotland* (1818), lived all his life at Whitley Hall, near Birdbrook, in Essex. On coming in to his inheritance, Walford began to embellish the estate with ornamental plantations (such as a flower garden with exotic shrubs and flowers and a collection of rare English plants) and buildings (notably a Temple of Floris). One of the visitors to the estate was the novelist and topographer James Norris Brewer, who described

> a wood of about seven acres, laid out in pleasant walks, and orna-
> mented with various seats and buildings. One of them, called the her-
> mitage, agreeably situated amongst the trees, consists of three circular
> apartments. It is built with wrag-stone, timber, and the bark of trees:
> the whole covered with thatch, paved with pebbles and tiles, and rus-
> ticated with moss, & c.

The information in this account is consistent with the images of the hermitage in an engraving in *Beauties of England and Wales* and in a coloured drawing of 1796 now in the Essex Record Office. Walford was a lifelong bachelor, so the figures in the foreground of the engraving are unlikely to be a family group, but may represent Walford entertaining two couples at his hermitage.

Across the Thames in Kent lies Mereworth Castle. The house is not a castle, but rather a fine copy of Palladio's Villa Rotonda, just

HERMITAGE in WHITLEY WOOD,
Essex.

FIGURE 4.17 Hermitage in Whitley Wood, Essex.

outside Vicenza. The 'Castle' was designed in 1723 by Colen Campbell for John Fane, seventh earl of Westmorland. It is so thoroughly
Palladian that Horace Walpole (who visited in 1752) felt obliged to
concede that the house was 'so perfect in the Palladian taste that it
has recovered me a little from the Gothic'. The park was landscaped,
and a series of elegant pavilions and lodges was constructed. One of
these buildings was a rustic hermitage, of which Walpole said nothing: he disapproved of hermitages, and may not have noticed this
Gothic intrusion into the architectural landscape. Little is known
of the hermitage save that it was inscribed with verses by Gilbert
West entitled 'Father Francis's Prayer' (for text see pp. 46–7). It is
clear that this was the hermitage for which the verses were composed,
because in printed texts it is subtitled 'Written in Lord Westmorland's

Hermitage'. West also wrote an inscription to be placed 'on the cell' ('Beneath these moss-grown roots, this rustic cell . . .') and another to be placed 'in the cell' ('Sweet bird, that singst on yonder spray'); the latter became well known because it was set as a glee in four parts by the composer Samuel Webbe. Lord Westmorland's hermitage disappeared long ago, but continued awareness of West's poems by students of the poetry of the period has ensured that its memory has not been extinguished.

The Gildredge estate, in Eastbourne (East Sussex), was the home of the Gilbert family from 1679 till 1923. In 1792 the proprietor of the estate was Nicholas Gilbert. In the same year his brother (and fellow lawyer) Charles, who lived in nearby Lewes, bought from Sir Stephen Lushington the manor house adjoining the Gildredge estate. Nicholas Gilbert died in 1797, and his brother Charles inherited his brother's half of the Gildredge estate. He moved into the Lushington mansion and sold the contents of the Gildredge manor house, which after partial demolition became a farm house. The hermitage, which still stands in what were the gardens of the adjoining Lushington mansion, was probably commissioned by Charles Gilbert rather than by Sir Stephen Lushington (as is sometimes assumed), because it was Charles who developed and extended the gardens at Lushington. The hermitage is an octagonal building in a Gothic idiom; the conical roof was originally thatched, and surmounted with a spiked and petalled finial (see Plate 7). Each of the five front bays has ogee-arched architraves with Gothic quatrefoils on either side of the peak; the three rear bays each has a bow (surmounted by a copper roof, formerly thatched) corresponding to a niche inside. The bays that flank the doorway have panelled bases, but the top half of each panel is a bottom-hinged shutter which opens outwards to reveal ogee-headed sashes which were once fitted with decorative glazing bars. Inside there is a board lining, a dado rail, and decorative bush garlands. The original furnishings are listed in an inventory of 1816 (occasioned by the death of Charles Gilbert), and are said to have included shells, fossils, a telescope, two conversation stools, grape glasses (i.e. rustic glasses with bubbles on the side), and a ewe sheep in a glass case. The purpose of the sheep is not altogether clear; perhaps the imagined hermit was also a shepherd, but it is also possible that the hermitage was being used to store an unwanted stuffed sheep.

Sometime during the first decade of the nineteenth century Charles Gilbert commissioned views of the gardens from Thomas Poppleton, who may be the man of the same name who had emigrated to the United States by 1810 and laid out the Baltimore grid in 1823. One of these colour-wash pictures, which are now in the East Sussex Record Office, includes a small image of the hermitage (from the north-east) in its original setting, with woods and hills behind and an open field in front. The manor house is not visible through the trees, which means that the hermitage was not visible from the house, but was rather secluded in trees. A note on the painting written by Mary Anne Gilbert (who had inherited the estate from her uncle in 1816) records that Mr Davies Gilbert (her husband, later president of the Royal Society) had removed the footpath to the south side of the Hermitage and placed over the arch a stone crop brought by him from Cornwall in 1817.

By the 1980s the hermitage had suffered interwar municipal decoration (including a pebble-dashed exterior and a copper roof), and subsequent dereliction. In 1990, as a nearby plaque attests, the hermitage was restored. The building is now roofed with thatch, and a door has been fitted, so this important survival is now both present-able and secure, and indeed is a very attractive feature of the public garden in which it is set.

Goodwood, which is now associated with historic motor racing, has been the Sussex seat of the dukes of Richmond for more than three centuries. The first duke, who was one of the dozen or so illegitimate children of King Charles II, bought Goodwood as a hunting lodge. The second duke engaged the architect Roger Morris to enlarge and restyle the house. Morris was responsible for garden buildings such as Carné's Seat (the banqueting house on the hill above the park), so it is possible that it was he who designed the small rubblestone hermitage for the garden, which was part of a menagerie complex in which the duke kept animals such as lions, tigers, leopards, tigers, bears, wolves, monkeys, and an armadillo. It seems that the hermitage was used to accommodate birds or other animals, so its purpose was not obviously contemplative. That said, a structure which consists of a vaulted cell with curved walls and two lantern niches seems to gesture in its design towards human habitation, but its precise status is unknown.

At the beginning of the eighteenth century Carshalton House (Surrey) was the property of John Radcliffe, the philanthropist and royal physician (and eponym of the Oxford buildings known as the Radcliffe Camera, the Radcliffe Observatory, and the Radcliffe Infirmary). On his death in 1714 the estate was bought by Sir John Fellowes, a director of the South Sea Company; when that Bubble burst in 1721, the house was confiscated, and thence passed to the Lord Chancellor, Philip Yorke, first Earl of Hardwicke. The house has had two gardens: the first was a landscape garden with a formal canal designed in about 1715 by Charles Bridgeman for Fellowes, and the second was a picturesque garden laid out by an unknown designer for Lord Hardwicke. The date of the hermitage is unknown, and it could be the work of either designer. Bridgeman was later to assist Queen Caroline to lay out Richmond Gardens, where William Kent designed a hermitage, but 1715 is too early for a hermitage. Lord Hardwicke's views on hermitages are not known, nor is he known to have taken much interest in Carshalton House (he never lived there); in 1749 his son, the second earl, built a root house at Wrest, and that might indicate a family interest in such buildings, but that is a very thin argument. My view is the building was probably constructed as part of the formal garden that Bridgeman designed for Fellowes, but that it was not at that stage identified as a hermitage. Indeed, as Andrew Skelton has remarked in his notes on the hermitage, the building is first referred to as a hermitage in a sale catalogue of 1815, which states that 'under a steep bank, is a hermitage, embowered in a grove of yew trees'.

Bridgeman's garden was designed to be viewed from the south front of the splendid Queen Anne mansion that still dominates the site. Looking straight ahead (south) from the mansion, the viewer saw the fine water tower that is the principal building in the garden. Looking at an angle to the right (south-west), the viewer saw the building now designated as the hermitage, with its façade directly facing the house. It was at this stage almost certainly a garden pavilion, a judgement that is consistent with its architecture: the building is a substantial architect-designed ashlar construction (made from Reigate stone), not a rusticated ruin or a root house. When the unknown garden designer employed by Lord Hardwicke created a picturesque garden, yew trees were planted and the lake dug, and the pavilion was transformed into a hermitage overlooking one end of the lake; the path around the lake would take visitors past the hermitage. In the late nineteenth century the mansion became a school, and in 1893 it was acquired by the Daughters of the Cross, who created a spiritualized landscape in which the hermitage became one of the stations of the cross.

The hermitage is a complex building. The façade has five openings, of which the outer two are open windows and the inner three are open doorways. The façade is extended in both directions by knapped flint walls added in the nineteenth century. Inside there are vaulted stone passages and a substantial circular chamber, which is vented. There is some evidence that this was initially an icehouse. When the building came to be designated as a hermitage, the chamber would have become the hermit's cell. In 1920, as part of the refashioning of the site to reflect the spirituality of the religious order, the chamber became an oratory. The building has thus fulfilled three very different functions, the second of which was that of ornamental hermitage. The building is now maintained by the Carshalton Water Tower & Historic Garden Trust, which cares for other follies on the site, notably the water tower (a former bath house) and a folly bridge (actually a dam). The iron railings that now protect the building were installed in 1993.

These are the English hermitages of which sufficient is known (at least by me) to be included here. Others have a more ghostly existence. In Ware Park (Hertford), for example, there is a ruined hermitage said in the Listed Buildings Register to have been built in the seventeenth century; this seems unlikely, but in the absence of documentation it is difficult to gainsay this judgement. The likelihood is

FIGURE 4.18 The hermitage, Carshalton.

that hermitages were to be found in most landscape gardens, but most have crumbled into oblivion.

A postscript: the Victorian hermitage

With the accession of Queen Victoria the hermitage moved out of the gloomy woodlands of England into the intermittent sunshine of the lawns. One fine example of this shift in sensibility is the hermitage at Bicton House (near East Budleigh, Devon). It was commissioned by Louisa, Lady Rolle (wife of the politician John, Lord Rolle), in 1839, at the beginning of Queen Victoria's reign. The hermitage, which overlooks a tiny canal, is a wood and brick octagon flanked on either side by a pavilion with gables supported by tree trunks. The exterior is covered with tiny wooden fishtail shingles, as is the two-tier pyramid roof. The windows are glazed with irregular patterns of

FIGURE 4.19 The hermitage, Bicton House.

stained glass, apparently taken from older windows. Inside, the floor is constructed of sheep's knucklebones and the walls of basket-weave wicker-work; both features had long been out of fashion, so the building is deliberately anachronistic. The rustic fireplace is surmounted by the Rolle arms. Furniture consists of an octagonal table patterned with strips of wood and rustic chairs. The style of the building is retrospective and archaic, a gentle gesture towards the past. It marks the point at which the garden hermitage ceased to gesture towards sombre reflection or even to accommodate a hermit, and instead became an elegant garden building that looked back towards a romantic age. The building is well maintained, thanks to the conscientious work of the Bicton Park Botanical Gardens, to which it now belongs. These capacious gardens have a miniature railway, and one of the stops is called 'Hermitage'; the Bicton hermitage is unique among hermitages in having its own railway station.

Bicton's hermitage is very fine, but soon less distinguished examples began to appear, often built by contractors such as James Pulham and Son, who are best known for rock gardens (including one in the garden of Buckingham Palace) but also provided garden buildings such as hermitages. The age of the English hermitage had passed, though, as will become apparent in Chapter 6, there has been a minor revival in our own time.

5

The Hermitage in the Celtic Lands

The ornamental hermit and his hermitage are in their origins English, but the English landscape garden and its hermitages spread beyond the borders of England to Ireland and Scotland. There are apparently no hermitages in Wales, though there are two shell grottoes said to have been built by hermits. The interior of the Cilwendeg Shell House near Boncath (Pembrokeshire), built in the late 1820s for Morgan Jones the Younger and wonderfully restored in 2004, has a patterned floor made from the knucklebones of sheep, and walls decorated with seashells, rocks, and glass fragments that have been pressed into lime mortar panels. Similarly, the shell grotto near Pontypool (Gwent) commissioned by the ironmaster John Hanbury in 1830 and completed in 1844 by his son Capel is said to have been built by a hermit whose building accomplishments included the patterned bone floor and walls and ceiling festooned with bark and stones and stalactites. Despite the contribution of perpetually evasive hermits, these buildings are clearly grottoes rather than hermitages.

Ireland

Hermitages in the English tradition were often built in Ireland, where they are said to be found on demesnes rather than on estates. The term 'demesne' is used in two distinctive ways in Ireland, sometimes as a collective term for the scattered estates of a single landowner (such as Viscount Kenmare), but more commonly as a term to denote a designed landscape associated with a country house.

The transplanting of the English landscape garden to Ireland was one of the many achievements of Mary Delany, the wife of Patrick Delany, the dean of Down. Mrs Delany was long known primarily as a letter-writer, and in 1761 George Montague (soon to be the fourth duke of Manchester) compared her epistolary skills to those of Madame de Sévigné; it is hard to imagine higher praise. More recently her many accomplishments in the decorative arts (particularly botanical illustration, but also painting in oil and watercolour, drawing, and the shellwork decoration of grottoes) have received proper recognition, notably in the 'Mrs Delany and her Circle' exhibition mounted at the Yale Center for British Art in 2009 and at Sir John Soane's Museum in 2010. This exhibition demonstrated the very high quality of Mrs Delany's art. Had she chosen to work in the fine arts rather than the decorative arts, she would rightly be accorded high standing amongst Britain's artists.

In Ireland Mrs Delany created two gardens, one at Downpatrick (seat of her husband's deanery) and the other at Delville (where her husband had established a garden in 1719). Delville was a small demesne in the parish of Glasnevin, near Dublin on the site of what is now the Bons Secours Hospital. It was at Delville that Mrs Delany became a *salonière* for the Ascendancy of Ireland. The gardens at

Delville were relatively small (11 acres/4.5 hectares), given the size of the house, and some visitors wrote teasingly about this. The actor Thomas Sheridan, for example, wrote 'A Description of Dr Delany's Villa':

> You scarce upon the borders enter
> Before you're at the very centre.

He did, however, concede that much was packed into the garden. There was a temple, for which Jonathan Swift wrote the epitaph on the frieze (*Fastigia descipit urbis*: I look down on the city's roofs); the interior was decorated with shells and pebbles, and furnished with busts of Swift and 'Stella' (Swift's friend Esther Johnson). Swift was a regular visitor to the garden, and his own garden, called 'Naboth's Vineyard' with reference to the bloody tale told in 1 Kings 21, seems to have exercised some influence on Delville.

At Delville, which drew on the *ferme ornée* tradition, Mrs Delany built a root-house hermitage known as the 'Beggar's Hut' which was little more than a shelter for a seat, created by enlarging a natural cave. This alcove was the image of retirement from the tainted urban world to an edenic world in which virtue was protected. An album of Mrs Delany's drawings now in the National Gallery of Ireland contains an image of her Delville garden that accentuates the intimacy that she hoped guests would feel by placing the hermitage with its little bench at the centre of the composition.

Mrs Delany's benign influence radiated to demesnes in all four of the historic provinces of Ireland. I shall survey those of which I am aware province by province: first, there are six more demesnes around Dublin and elsewhere in the historic province of Leinster; second, there are six demesnes in Ulster, all of which are now in Northern Ireland; third, there is a single demesne in Connacht;

FIGURE 5.1 Mary Delany, pen and ink drawing of her garden at Delville.

fourth, there are two demesnes in Munster, including the only one with a Roman Catholic proprietor.

The earliest known hermitage in Leinster after Mrs Delany's was the work of the Irish politician Gustavus Handcock, who in 1725 married the heiress Elizabeth Temple, and as a condition of inheriting her Waterstown demesne (near Athlone, County Westmeath) changed his name to Gustavus Handcock-Temple. In 1745 Handcock-Temple commissioned the Hiberno-German architect Richard Castle to build a new house on the demesne to replace the medieval castle. The surrounding gardens were landscaped, and the buildings in the landscape included a substantial stone hermitage cut into a hill high above an artificial lake. The hermitage, which was erected c.1780, was once surrounded by trees, but, as a nearby plaque explains, much of the timber on the demesne was destroyed by a hurricane on 6 January 1839. The main house was abandoned in 1923 and has now gone, except for a few walls, but the hermitage is still standing, albeit in a ruinous roofless state. It has the vestiges of a pedimented façade topped by a finial, and three pointed arches for a door and flanking windows; each of the three openings is decorated with large stones. Inside there was a single rectangular room, apparently plastered, with a fireplace and niches in the rear wall. It must have been a quiet, comfortable space, and certainly provided fine views across the countryside, as it still does.

In the same period, another hermitage was constructed in Leinster by James Caufeild, first earl of Charlemont, whose suburban villa was called Marino House. The demesne is now known for the Casino, a garden house designed by Sir William Chambers for Lord Charlemont and built in the third quarter of the eighteenth century; it is surely Ireland's finest neoclassical building. In the same grounds, Lord Charlemont also built

FIGURE 5.2 The hermitage, Waterstown, County Westmeath.

159

a root house, of which little is now known. Its physical appearance, however, is known from a drawing by Thomas Sautelle Roberts in the National Gallery of Ireland. It was clearly a substantial root house.

Within a few years of Lord Charlemont's construction of Marino House, the politician John Foster, first Baron Oriel, inherited the demesne of Oriel Temple, in Collon, County Louth; it is named after a garden house (in the form of a Doric temple) in the grounds of Collon House, the home of the politician Anthony Foster, who was John Foster's father. The younger Foster decided to convert the garden house into a full-scale residence. Construction of the 'Temple' began in 1780. The house survives, and has what seems to be the earliest Doric portico in Ireland. It is now a Trappist monastery known as New Mellifont Abbey.

The Fosters built several follies, including a grotto (now gone), a rustic cottage (now modernized), and an ornamental hermitage (see Plate 8). The hermitage, which is now derelict, overlooks a lake (now partly obscured by trees) in a part of the gardens that still retains features of the late eighteenth-century landscape garden. It is a rectangular building made with rough stone, including tufa and lumps of marble; entry is through a small side doorway with niches on either side. Inside there are two rooms, each with a domed ceiling. The first room is circular, and is fitted with a fireplace and with niches for seats; it is lit by means of a large Gothic window opening. At the rear of this room an opening leads to a D-shaped room with another large Gothic window opening. In both rooms the floors consist of pebbles arranged in patterns. The building was presumably used by the Foster family for social gatherings. In its present state, it is not possible to judge whether the building was furnished in ways meant to imply that a hermit was in residence.

Luttrellstown is a 400-acre (160-hectare) heavily wooded demesne on the banks of the River Liffey, four miles from Dublin on the road to Lucan. The demesne is so called from its first proprietor, Simon Luttrell, first earl of Carhampton. It was his son, the soldier and politician Henry Lawes Luttrell, second earl of Carhampton, who developed the already dramatic landscape into one that realized his romantic ideals. One feature in the landscape was a building which was described in a letter of 14 August 1828 by Prince Hermann von Pückler-Muskau:

> I must mention a curious 'pavillon rustique' which is built in a suitable spot in the 'pleasure ground.' It is hexagonal, three sides solid, and fashioned of pieces of rough branches of trees very prettily arranged in various patterns; the other three consist of two windows and a door. The floor is covered with a mosaic of little pebbles from the brook, the ceiling with shells, and the roof is thatched with wheat straw on which the full ears are left.

He is clearly describing a hermitage. Indeed, one of the plates in Jonathan Fisher's *Scenery of Ireland* (1795) is labelled 'The wooden bridge at Hermitage on the River Liffey', and the hermitage can be seen close to the bridge. The castle and demesne survive, and have been refashioned as a luxury resort, perhaps best known as the setting for the wedding of Victoria Adams and David Beckham. There are, alas, no wedding photographs of Victoria and David at the hermitage, because it disappeared long ago. Lord Carhampton subsequently bought Painshill, in Surrey, and with it the hermitage that Charles Hamilton had constructed.

The last hermitage to be built in Leinster before the modern one at the National Stud was St Enda's Hermitage, in a suburb of Dublin. In the sixth century St Enda founded a monastery at Tighlagheany, on Inishmore, the largest of the Aran Islands. The monastic remains

FIGURE 5.3 Jonathan Fisher, 'The wooden bridge at Hermitage on the River Liffey'.

there are authentic, but the Hermitage of St Enda in Dublin is ornamental, and was not associated with St Enda until the early twentieth
century. This stone building is in the grounds of an eighteenth-
century house originally known as the Fields of Odin in Rathfarnham, County Dublin. Early in the nineteenth century the house was
bought by Edward Hudson, a society dentist and polymath who
practised in Dublin's Grafton Street. He renamed the house, calling
it 'The Hermitage', and set about populating the gardens with follies,
including druidic standing stones, towers, a fort, a ruined abbey, and
a hermitage. The hermitage was constructed from large crude stones
set in what appears to be a rocky outcrop in a woodland clearing.
Inside, there is one large room with a door and a window opening.
The room has an arched recess with a stone bench, and a small niche.

FIGURE 5.4 St Enda's Hermitage, Dublin.

In front is an imitation dolmen which doubled as the druid's altar and a picnic table.

The association with St Enda arose in 1910, when Patrick Pearse moved his bilingual secondary boarding school for boys from Ranelagh to Rathfarnham. The school in Ranelagh had been called St Enda's, and the name travelled with the boys to the new location. Pearse was a formidable educationalist, but the school depended heavily on his personal charisma as a fundraiser, so his execution in May 1916 for his part in the Easter Rising set it on a downward slope to eventual closure in 1935; it is now a Pearse Museum, dedicated to Patrick and his brother Willie, who was also executed (together with 15 former pupils of the school).

The hand of Mrs Delany extended to Ulster through her friendship with Lord and Lady Orrery. John Boyle, fifth earl of Cork and fifth earl of Orrery, was a friend of Pope and Swift who had addressed the problem of his burden of debt by marrying an Irish heiress. It was at Lady Orrery's demesne in the village of Caledon in County Tyrone (now in Northern Ireland) that Lord Orrery constructed a root house in 1746. As he explained in a letter to his chaplain, 'we have built, at the expense of five pounds, a root house, or hermitage, to which on Sunday the country people resort, as the Londoners to Westminster Abbey'. Mary Delany's residence for part of each year in Downpatrick afforded an opportunity to inspect the Caledon garden, where, as she described in a letter of 1748, she saw

> a hermitage, which is about an acre of ground—an island, planted with all variety of trees, shrubs and flowers that will grow in this country, abundance of little winding walks, differently embellished with little seats and banks; in the midst is placed a hermit's cell, made of the roots of trees, the floor is paved with pebbles, there is a couch made of matting, and little wooden stools, a table with a manuscript on it, a pair of spectacles, a leathern bottle; and hung up in different parts, an hourglass, a weatherglass and several mathematical instruments, a shelf of books, another of wood platters and bowls, another of earthen ones, in short everything that you might imagine necessary for a recluse.

And who was the hermit? At times it was an imagined hermit who had momentarily absented himself, leaving his personal belongings on the table; at other times Lord Orrery assumed the role himself. In a letter to his friend Richard Pococke written in 1748 he said that

> Thomson's *Castle of Indolence* came to me last post. I have not read it yet. Such a poem will certainly be very proper to my hermitage, which is now in such beauty that I am impatient to see you there.

Whenever they were apart Lord and Lady Orrery wrote to each other, and their affectionate correspondence is one of the delights of eighteenth-century literature. Lady Orrery repeatedly refers to her husband as 'my Laelius', with reference to his capacity for friendship (the friendship of Caius Laelius and Scipio Africanus was immortalized by Cicero in his dialogue on friendship, *De Amicitia*). In the summer of 1748 she wrote to her absent husband with news of progress on the hermitage:

> Yesterday being the day after the fair, there was little work done; red nose Stow absent, John not busy, Joans inactive, scarce a man at the Hermitage, of which place I can give no account, for I have not been there since my Laelius left his paradise; but if the weather is better this afternoon I will make it a visit, and you shall know on Saturday whether the fair has destroyed all the industry of the week.

The 'paradise' is an allusion to Adam's hut (see p. 41). In a letter written a few days later Lady Orrery describes her determination that three visiting judges 'should see my Laelius's charming works'. She therefore organized 'coaches and post-chaises' to take them to the hermitage, and reported that on seeing it 'they were in raptures'. When abroad Lord Orrery sometimes assumed the persona of the hermit. Writing to his wife from London, he asked her to 'pity a poor hermit and send me some news'. A man who rejoiced in friendship inevitably enjoyed the company of other hermits: a letter from Lord Bolingbroke assured Lord Orrery that 'whenever you can come hither you will give great pleasure to the hermits of the place'.

In the mid-eighteenth century, Tollymore House, in County Down, was the summer retreat of James Hamilton, Viscount Limerick (later first earl of Clanbrassil). Lord Limerick became the principal Irish patron of Thomas Wright, who worked as a landscape designer at Lord Limerick's main residence, at Dundalk (Louth). The buildings that he constructed there included what Richard

Pococke (Church of Ireland bishop, and traveller in Egypt and the Levant) described as a 'thatched open house supported by bodies of fir trees', which sounds like one of Wright's arbours, some of which are designated as hermitages. There is similar uncertainty about Wright's role at Tollymore Park, which he visited in the summer of 1746, but he may have been responsible for what Pococke described in 1752 as 'a thatched open place to dine in, which is very romantic, with a stove near to prepare the entertainment'; this building (which has now disappeared) is designated on a map of 1777 as the 'old hermitage'.

It is possible that one of the factors that influenced the decision to build a hermitage was Lord Limerick's recollection of his grand tour, when, as he recorded in his diary, he saw the hermitages at Fontainebleau in May 1716, a few months after the death of Louis XIV:

> Louis built three hermitages in the forest; one of them was pulled down by reason of the hermit being murdered there. The other two are still standing, both of which I saw. The late king used to give entertainment to the ladies at one of them that is situated in the wildest place that can be imagined.

This is a problematical entry, not least because Louis XIV did not build any hermitages at Fontainebleau; his were at Marly. As for hermitages being pulled down, there may be confusion with the destruction of Port-Royal des Champs (close to Versailles) in 1709–10, when the nuns were expelled and the buildings razed. The murdered hermit adds still more confusion, as this was a folk myth (or a true story from the medieval period) associated with the hermitage at Franchard, a real hermitage which is indeed in the Forest of Fontainebleau. Here is Robert Louis Stevenson's account in his short story 'Merry Men' (1882):

'Have you been to Franchard, Jean-Marie?' inquired the Doctor. 'I fancy not.'

'Never,' replied the boy.

'It is a ruin in a gorge,' continued Desprez, adopting his expository voice; 'the ruin of a hermitage and chapel. History tells us much of Franchard; how the recluse was often slain by robbers; how he lived on a most insufficient diet; how he was expected to pass his days in prayer.'

The fact that Lord Limerick's diary entry is a tissue of garbled memories is not of consequence. What matters is that his 'recollections' may have inspired him to build the first hermitage at Tollymore.

Lord Limerick died in 1758, by which time he had become earl of Clanbrassil. His son, also James Hamilton, who became the second earl of Clanbrassil, accelerated the process of creating a romantic garden at Tollymore. The rugged setting was ideal for such a garden. As Sir Richard Colt Hoare commented, 'few, if any, noblemen, either in Ireland or in the sister kingdom, can boast of a residence placed in so singular and romantic a situation'. The second Lord Clanbrassil commissioned a series of ornamental buildings for his demesne, including a barbican gate (the Bryansford Gate, dated 1786), a barn (the Clanbrassil Barn) which looks like a church, and a hermitage.

The main house was demolished in 1952, but the gate, the barn, and the hermitage all survive, and are now in the care of the Forest Service of Northern Ireland. The hermitage, above the Shimna River, is constructed of stone (see Plate 9). It is approached from the river footpath, which close to the hermitage becomes a wooden platform with a rustic balustrade. The hermitage has a narrow entry from the footpath, and two Gothic openings overlooking a pool in the river. The principal room is some 2.4 by 3.7 metres. A smaller second room gives access to the beech woods above, and this may have been the original point of access to the hermitage. At the back of the main room a stone bench runs along the rock-face which forms the rear wall. There was a dated inscription on a plaque on the back wall (now removed), and if the inscription is contemporary with the rest of the building, it must have been constructed in 1770. The plaque read (in Greek) 'Clanbrassil, to his very dear friend Monthermer 1770'. 'Monthermer' was John Brudenell, son of the earl of Cardigan, and he was known by the courtesy title of marquess of Monthermer. He died on 11 April 1770 at the age of 35. The original furnishings of the hermitage included a bust of Lord Monthermer, but that has now gone. He was, however, painted in 1758 by Pompeo Batoni, while visiting Rome on his grand tour. The portrait passed by marriage from the earls of Cardigan to the dukes of Buccleuch, and now hangs at Boughton House, in Northamptonshire. It shows a young man marking his place with a finger as he looks up from a copy of Corelli's *Sonata for Violin*, no. 6 (Opus 5). The image may not be faithful in every detail (it would be difficult to play a violin sonata on the mandolin beside him), but it successfully conveys the image of a cultivated young man, and his death at such an early age made him a particularly appropriate subject for commemoration in a place such as a hermitage set aside for thoughtfulness.

In 1823 Alexander Atkindon recorded the impression that a visit to the Tollymore hermitage made on him:

> In this homely hermitage (the meditations of whose inhabitant are rendered solemn by the murmuring of the river), a stone bench, the full length of the enclosure, has been arranged for his couch or resting place. The planted hill, which forms the opposite bank of the river, confines the hermit's attention to the romantic scenery of his cell, and shuts out every foreign object, every illusive scene of that lower world to which he has bid adieu.

The imagined hermit is a powerful presence in the mind of the visitor.

Tollymore House was not the only Ulster demesne at which Thomas Wright worked in the mid-1740s. At Florence Court, the Fermanagh seat of the earls of Enniskillen, Wright seems to have been the designer of a hermitage thatched in heather. An image of this building survives in a photograph of 1860 of the third earl and his family. The demesne is now owned by the National Trust, which in 1992 commissioned a specialist company (Raffles Garden Buildings) to reconstruct the hermitage, which is now known as the Heather House. Then as now, the building overlooks the pleasure gardens and Ben Aughlin, and so functioned as a gazebo as well as a hermitage and a setting for family photographs.

There was at least one other hermitage in Fermanagh, at Belle Isle, on Upper Lough Erne. This was the island demesne of General Sir

FIGURE 5.5 Loughgall hermitage, Armagh.

Ralph Gore (sixth baronet, later Viscount Belleisle and then first Earl Ross). Sir Ralph laid out footpaths around the island, and built a temple and a grotto. He also built a thatched hermitage, which was described by Jonathan Fisher in his *Scenery of Ireland* (1795) as 'a handsome cottage with a kitchen and other conveniences, in a sweet retired part [of the demesne], secluded from the powerful influence of the sun during the summer months'. The siting of a building in Ireland to avoid the sun seems odd to a twenty-first-century visitor, but gloom was essential for the ambience of an ornamental hermitage.

The last eighteenth-century hermitage in Ulster was built in the grounds of Loughgall Manor House (Armagh), which was for 350 years the home of the Cope family. The hermitage, in a wooded area of the demesne, was constructed from limestone rubble which seems to emerge naturally from a rocky outcrop in a small clearing; some of the stones have been moulded by a river. The roof is covered with grassed soil. The narrow entrance doorway is arched, and now has a modern trellised steel door and frame. The interior has a domed roof and two windows. The building is difficult to date, especially as it appears on the Ordnance Survey map of 1860 but not on the OS map of 1834. In terms of style, however, it seems likely to have been built between 1790 and 1820. It is an excellent surviving example of a hermitage in the picturesque tradition, but nothing is known of its origins or use.

Greenmount, on the outskirts of Antrim, is now one of the three campuses of Northern Ireland's College of Agriculture, Food and Rural Enterprise. In the early nineteenth century Greenmount was the demesne of the Thompson family, of which little is known. The local aristocrat (Clotworthy Skeffington, earl of Massereene)

FIGURE 5.6 The Hermitage, Greenmount.

disparagingly referred to Robert Thompson (who built the present house in 1820) as 'farmer Thompson', but it is quite clear that the Thompsons were considerable landowners, with properties in Meath and Lowth as well as the small demesne in Antrim. In the early nineteenth century the property consisted of about 160 acres (65 hectares), of which 39 (16 hectares) were laid out as a landscape garden, and the rest used for farming.

In July 1809 a correspondent of the *Belfast Monthly Magazine* known only by initials (S.M.S.) published the second part of a 'sketch of a ramble to Antrim', in which he described how

> we crossed the fields to Greenmount, the elegant seat of ------- Thompson Esq., about one mile from Antrim, near the road leading to Muckamore. This beautiful villa stands on rising ground and is completely furnished in the modern taste; the demesne is planted with a great number of trees and shrubs laid out into some very pleasing walks. At the rear of the building are two small lakes, well stocked

with fish; on them also some swans. On the verge of one of the fore-
mentioned lakes, in a shrubbery, is a hermitage built with romantic
simplicity, and opposite is a small island, joined to the mainland by a
stonework arch.

Another visitor's impressions were published in *Ireland Exhibited to
England* in 1823:

> The lake which reflects the beauty of its glassy wave on this retired
> scene is surrounded by a thick plantation through which there is a
> sanded walk for the accommodation of the family of Greenmount
> and its visitors. In this group of beauties a very elegant hermitage
> offers its consolations to those strangers who wish to retire from the
> world and converse only with themselves.

The 'stonework arch' of the 1809 account survives, but the island
does not. The hermitage is assumed to have been lost, but may be
the building now described as the 'summer house'. It seems to have
been decorated with seashells, which would ordinarily imply a grotto
rather than a hermitage, but there is no record of a grotto at Greenmount. The hermitage is now roofless, and the lake that it overlooked
is now a swamp, but in its time it was clearly a very fine building.

The only surviving hermitage in the historic province of Connacht is
in the grounds of Kilronan Castle, an early nineteenth-century
Gothic castle near the village of Ballyfarnon (County Roscommon),
a few miles south-east of Sligo. Initially Kilronan was the home of the
King-Tennison family, and it was subsequently occupied by their
kinsmen the earls of Kingston. The Castle was in a ruined state in the
1990s, but has been restored and is now an elegant luxury hotel and
health spa. The lodge at the original entrance (now a staff entrance

FIGURE 5.7 The Hermitage, Kilronan Castle.

for the hotel) was originally designed as a hermitage. This double function is not altogether clear, but it seems likely that an ornamental hermitage in the grounds of an earlier house became a gate-keeper's lodge when Kilronan Castle was rebuilt in the nineteenth century. The building is constructed from river-worn stone, and is set into a bank that once overlooked the lake; the view is now obstructed by trees. Inside there are two rooms, both with fireplaces. The room on the right, which has a curved front wall, has an arched doorway, three windows, and a stone-flagged floor. From this room there is an entrance to a rectangular room on the left, which has a stone-flagged floor and traces of lime plaster. The finest feature is a loggia with 2.4-metre piers of contorted river rock. The hermitage is an eccentric combination of architectural features (notably pointed Gothic arches) and 'natural' features (the floor plan and the oddly shaped stones). The view overlooking the lake probably implies that it was used by the King-Tennison family for social occasions. This hermitage now lacks a roof, but seems otherwise solid; it is a remarkable survival.

There are two hermitages associated with Munster, both of exceptional interest. The one that survives, and indeed has only recently been recovered, is at Glin Castle, in County Limerick, which was the seat of the Knights of Glin for more than 700 years. The present castle was completed in 1780 by Colonel John Bateman FitzGerald, 23rd Knight of Glin, after which the gardens were laid out. His son, John Fraunceis FitzGerald, was only twelve when his father died in 1803 and he became the 24th Knight of Glin. He remained in England to

FIGURE 5.8 The hermitage, Glin Castle.

complete his education (Winchester and Cambridge), living during the vacations at Forde Abbey, his grandparents' home in Dorset. In England he seems to have adopted a romantic view of Ireland and his own family history, and on returning to Glin set about shaping the demesne to realize this vision. He castellated the mansion, built a Gothic gatehouse (in which he installed a mistress), and commissioned a series of garden buildings and structures, including a bathing lodge (an eye-catcher that looks like a miniature fort) and a hermitage. By the time he died in 1854, the fashion for garden hermitages had abated, and the hermitage gradually started to disappear under soil and brambles. It lay in this unloved state until a restoration programme was initiated in the 1970s by Desmond Fitzgerald, the 29th Knight of Glin, and his wife Olda Fitzgerald, both published garden historians with expertise in restoration. As part of this programme, the ornamental hermitage at Glin has recently been excavated and restored, and a circle of standing stones has been placed a few yards away. The hermitage is a small Gothic building with three arched openings; it contains a single room with a brick-vaulted coved ceiling and a pebbled floor. Its present setting, in a glade on the edge of an oak coppice, is true to the idea of the ornamental hermitage. Its original use is hard to judge; it seems too small for entertaining, and may have been no more than a pleasant place to sit, or to shelter from the rain.

The second hermitage in Munster was the work of Thomas Browne, fourth Viscount Kenmare, who in 1736 inherited a vast demesne of some 120,000 acres (50,000 hectares), mainly in County Kerry, but also in Limerick and Cork. His seat was at Kenmare House, near Killarney. Innisfallen Island, in nearby Lough Leane, was the site of a ruined abbey which was for centuries the home of a community of Augustinian Canons Regular. Lord Kenmare rebuilt part of the abbey ruins as a hermitage, and used it as a dining hall for entertaining. The hermitage was small, but sufficiently large to accommodate a servant who could serve wine through the windows to guests who could collect their salmon from a table outside. The spirit of these occasions seems likely to have been light-hearted, but cheerful melancholy was part of the purpose of any hermitage, even if it was serving as a bar. Thomas Moore tried to hint at this quality in 'Sweet Innisfallen', which he praised as a place

> Where erring man might hope to rest—
> Might hope to rest, and find in thee
> A gloom like Eden's, on the day
> He left its shade, when every tree,
> Like thine, hung weeping o'er his way.
> Weeping or smiling, lovely isle!
> And all the lovelier for thy tears.

The eremetical wine-waiter is difficult to interpret with confidence. It is striking that no other Georgian hermitage in Ireland is known to have accommodated a human hermit. The reason may be that most landowners were Protestant, but the locally available cheap labour was Catholic. Having a Catholic hermit installed in one's hermitage might imply a longing for the Old Faith, and that was not an impression that most landowners would have wanted to give. Lord Kenmare, however, was a determined Roman Catholic who repeatedly declined educational and political opportunities if they required him to renounce his faith. It seems possible that his hermitage and its apparently secular hermit hinted at the centuries when Ireland had religious hermits.

Scotland

There are five surviving Georgian hermitages in Scotland: two in Dumfriesshire (now Dumfries and Galloway), one near Edinburgh, and two in Perthshire. Both Dumfriesshire hermitages have associations with Robert Burns, and both Perthshire hermitages with the Wordsworths.

In the spring of 1788 Robert Burns trained as an excise officer and moved into a farm at Ellisland, on the River Nith north of Dumfries. There he worked as a dairy farmer and as an exciseman, but also found time to write poetry (notably 'Tam o' Shanter') and to adapt traditional Scottish poems, including 'My Heart's in the Highlands' and 'Auld Lang Syne'. Some of Burns's neighbours were puzzled by the arrival of a poet (Burns said that they had 'as much idea of a rhinoceros as of a poet'), but one friendship proved to be particularly productive. Ellisland abutted onto Glenriddell, the estate of the antiquary, amateur musician, and literary patron Robert Riddell. The estate is now Friars Carse, a country house hotel. Burns prepared for Riddell a two-volume collection of his unpublished poems and letters (now in the National Library of Scotland). In the woods at the southern end of his estate, a few yards from Ellisland, Riddell had built a hermitage and a druids' circle. Riddell gave Burns a key to enable him to meditate and compose in the hermitage whenever he chose. On 28 June 1788 Burns wrote the first version of the poem now known as 'Verses in Friars' Carse Hermitage'. He is said to have engraved the first twelve lines on one of the window panes:

> Thou whom chance may hither lead,
> Be thou clad in russet weed,

FIGURE 5.9 Friars Carse Burns Hermitage.

Be thou decked in silken stole,
Grave these counsels on thy soul.
Life is but a day at most,
Sprung from night, in darkness lost;
Hope not sunshine every hour.
Fear not clouds will always lour.
As Youth and Love with sprightly dance
Beneath thy morning star advance,
Pleasure with her siren air
May delude the thoughtless pair.

The window pane is no longer in the hermitage, which after Riddell's death fell into disrepair, but the building was restored in 1874 and is now in good repair. The hermitage, which is approached along an avenue of yews in the woodland, is a small rectangular gabled building constructed from red sandstone rubble with polished dressings; the interior is fitted with a fireplace. Burns was a Mason, and in the course of the Victorian restoration Masonic symbols were carved into the south wall of the exterior. The hermitage was thus transformed into a memorial of Burns, and indeed is now known as the Friars Carse Burns Hermitage. Ellisland is now a Burns museum, and visitors can walk across the fields into the woodland where the hermitage is preserved by the Friars Carse Hotel. Of all the hermitages described in this book, Friars Carse has the most important literary associations, for the contemplative atmosphere that it provided gave rise to some of the most famous poems of Scotland's national poet.

FIGURE 5.10 The hermitage, Craigieburn.

Craigieburn, near Moffat, also has associations with Burns, because Craigieburn House was the birthplace of Jean Lorimer, Burns's 'Chloris'. Burns wrote a song about his experience of Craigieburn Wood ('Sweet fa's the eve on Craigieburn, | And blythe awakes the morrow') in which he declares that if the lady of his heart's affections refuses him, the leaves of Craigieburn will wither on his grave. The first pleasure gardens at Craigieburn were laid out in 1796 (the year in which Burns died), and it was in this period that a hermitage was constructed on a wooded bank high above Craigie Burn. The original garden fell into decline, but a magnificent new garden (with a Himalayan theme) has been created in its stead, and is open to the public. Throughout this process the setting of the hermitage has been preserved, and is recognizably the same as the copperplate engraving of the view from the ravine by the landscape painter and photographer David Octavius Hill in 1837. The hermitage is a small gabled chamber with a slated roof. The chamber, which has a vaulted stone ceiling, is lit by a small window, and would provide enough space for one person to sit comfortably. Entry is through a Gothic door with an asymmetrically pointed head. The building is made of rubble that has been rendered with 'Roman cement', the proprietary term for a hydraulic cement (unrelated to ancient Roman concrete) developed by Robert Parker in the 1780s (and patented in 1796) as an alternative to lime mortar, which was susceptible to water. This cement, which was produced by firing septaria taken from riverine clay, hardens in water, and so contributed to the excellent state of preservation of the Craigieburn hermitage.

Dalkeith Palace, a few miles from Edinburgh, was for centuries the principal seat of the dukes of Buccleuch. Nothing is known of the

FIGURE 5.11 The hermitage, Dalkeith Park.

history of the hermitage in Dalkeith Park, but it is likely to be the work of Henry Scott, third duke of Buccleuch and fifth duke of Queensberry, and his duchess, Lady Elizabeth. They moved into Dalkeith in 1767 and remained there until the duke's death in 1812. When the duke and duchess arrived, the palace and gardens were in a decaying state, and the improvements that they initiated seem likely to have included the hermitage, a rubble structure with a single barrel-vaulted room lit by a single window (now infilled) at the rear. There has been some restoration, notably a modern timber beam behind the doorway lintel, but the building is now a ruin, hidden in woodland beside a track on the estate. Nothing is known of its use, but it is too small for entertaining, and so was probably a quiet place for reflection and a refuge from the rain.

The rugged landscapes of Perthshire were well suited to the natural settings required for ornamental hermitages. In 1757 John Murray, the second duke of Atholl, built a hermitage on a rocky outcrop above the Black Linn Falls on the River Braan, a tributary of the Tay in Perthshire; in another version of the story, it was secretly built by a nephew as a surprise present (see Plate 10). The site was close to one of his residences, Dunkeld House. Mary Ann Hanway described a visit in her account published in 1776: the hermitage, she explains,

> is a neat pavilion, whose windows are formed of painted glass, through which you see the river falling from a surprising height into the horrid gulf beneath, with a most terrifying noise; and that which adds greatly to the formidable grandeur of the scene is that by looking through a part of the window which is red, it appears to be sheets of liquid fire rolling down the rock like the lava of Mount Etna. My ideas were so lively in picturing such images of horror that I was obliged to turn from indulging them, or from further contemplating the scene.

Painted glass was often a feature of hermitages, thanks to Milton's 'dim religious light', but at Dunkeld it was turned to the less contemplative purpose of evoking horror in the mind of the viewer.

Dunkeld House no longer exists, but the hermitage, constructed in a neoclassical style, still stands, now in the care of the National Trust for Scotland. It is, however, not quite in its original form, because in 1783 the hermitage was refashioned as a shrine to Ossian by the fourth duke of Atholl (another John Murray), and it is in this form that it has been restored after the unhappy depredations of the nineteenth century, when vandals set it alight (1821) and blew it up (1869) with dynamite, which had just come onto the market.

James Macpherson's poems of Ossian achieved something akin to cult status in the late eighteenth century, despite the insistence of English detractors (based on a sense of intellectual property not shared in Scotland) that they were forgeries. It is arguably more sensible to see the poems as Macpherson's mediation between the Gaelic and Anglophone cultures of Scotland. In 1783 Macpherson was still alive, living largely in London and serving as a member of parliament for a Cornish seat, and the Ossian poems had achieved a life and a standing that were largely independent of their author. A hermitage dedicated to Ossian was therefore unproblematical, and indeed created great interest amongst both Scots (who valued the military exploits) and English (who valued the elegiac and melancholic tone of the poems). Eminent visitors included the Wordsworths, J. M. W. Turner, and Felix Mendelssohn.

Visitors delighted in the painting of Ossian serenading maidens, and recoiled in happy horror at the 'hall of mirrors' that was revealed when the guide triggered a device that removed the painting and opened the way to a mirror-lined room in which it seemed that the Black Linn Falls fell down on all the surrounding walls. Dorothy Wordsworth recorded the scene in her *Recollections of a Tour Made in Scotland (1803)*, which is written in the form of a journal:

> The waterfall (which we came to see) warned us by a loud roaring that we must expect it; we were first, however, conducted into a small apartment, where the gardener desired us to look at a painting of the figure of Ossian, which, while he was telling us the story of the young artist who performed the work, disappeared, parting in the middle, flying asunder as if by the touch of magic, and lo! we are at the entrance of a splendid room, which was almost dizzy and alive with waterfalls, that tumbled in all directions—the great cascade, which was opposite to the window that faced us, being reflected in

> innumerable mirrors upon the ceiling and against the walls. We both laughed heartily, which, no doubt, the gardener considered as high commendation; for he was very eloquent in pointing out the beauties of the place.

This mildly hostile account is echoed by Dorothy's brother William, who wrote a not-very-good poem on the subject, condemning the hermitage as an 'intrusive Pile, ill-graced | With baubles of theatric taste' from which he withdrew fastidiously. In a prefatory note he added cruelly that

> I am not aware that this condemnatory effusion was ever seen by the owner of the place. He might be disposed to pay little attention to it; but were it to prove otherwise I should be glad, for the whole exhibition is distressingly puerile.

The mocking laughter of the Wordsworths and their wish to humiliate the creator of the hermitage are unattractive. The hermitage was restored in 2007, when sliding panels, a hidden handle, and mirrors were installed to re-create the effects intended by the original designers. The superior sneering of the Wordsworths is not echoed by twenty-first-century visitors, who delight in the special effects.

The estates of John Campbell, third earl of Breadalbane and Holland (whose daughter Jemima, Lady Grey, had built a hermitage at Wrest), included the Falls of Acharn, in Perthshire. In the 1760s Lord Breadalbane commissioned the construction of an octagonal hermitage overlooking the waterfall. Access to this room was through two dark and twisting tunnels. Visitors included Robert Burns and the Wordsworths. Dorothy Wordsworth wrote in her *Recollections* that

Having climbed perhaps a quarter of a mile, we were conducted into a locked-up plantation, and guessed by the sound that we were near the cascade, but could not see it. Our guide opened a door, and we entered a dungeon-like passage, and, after walking some yards in total darkness, found ourselves in a quaint apartment stuck over with moss, hung about with stuffed foxes and other wild animals, and ornamented with a library of wooden books covered with old leather backs, the mock furniture of a hermit's cell. At the end of the room, through a large bow-window, we saw the waterfall.

The stone tunnels, which have recently been restored, are in the shape of a capital Y, with entrances at the tips of the two angled lines. The downward line, from the point where the two tunnels meet to the exit into the hermitage, is furnished with stone seats and a fireplace. At the bottom of the Y the visitor emerges into the light of an octagonal room that no longer has stuffed animals and a mock library, nor even a roof, but does afford a fine view of the falls and the

FIGURE 5.12 The hermitage, Falls of Acharn.

gorge leading down to Loch Tay. It is, as Dorothy said, 'a very beautiful prospect'. The hermit may have been imaginary, but he nonetheless provided an experience that pleased Dorothy and can still give pleasure to visitors.

In Scotland the transition from the Georgian hermitage (a small remote building designed to elicit strong emotions) to the Victorian hermitage (a fine garden building near the house) can be seen in a second hermitage built by the Campbells of Breadalbane. In 1834 John Campbell, the second marquess of Breadalbane, engaged James Gillespie Graham to enlarge and gothicize Taymouth Castle, in Kenmore, a few miles from the Falls of Acharn. Work was largely was completed by September 1842, when Queen Victoria visited. She wrote approvingly of her reception in her diary:

FIGURE 5.13 The hermitage, Taymouth Castle.

There were a number of Lord Breadalbane's Highlanders, all in the Campbell tartan, drawn up in front of the house, with Lord Breadalbane himself in a Highland dress at their head.... The firing of the guns, the cheering of the great crowd, the picturesqueness of the dresses, the beauty of the surrounding country, with its rich background of wooded hills, altogether formed one of the finest scenes imaginable. It seemed as if a great chieftain in olden feudal times was receiving his sovereign. It was princely and romantic.

The landscape that Lord Breadalbane created contained a number of follies, including rustic lodges supported by trees, miniature castles, and a rusticated hermitage across the river (spanned by a Chinese bridge) from the castle. The stone hermitage is a Gothic building consisting of a capacious rectangular room with a circular tower at one end. It survives in a ruined state, but its future, like that of Taymouth Castle, is uncertain, because the company that had embarked on the Castle's transformation into the UK's first six-star hotel went bankrupt in 2009, and all work stopped; a new owner is now at work on the Castle with a view to reopening in 2014.

The Afterlife of the Hermit

One might have thought that the garden hermit had had his day, which ended when fashion and sensibility changed and abolitionist sentiment discouraged the keeping of hermits. As we have seen, the hermit lived on in attenuated form as a fortune teller in a pleasure ground, albeit shorn of the ideology that underlay the phenomenon of the Georgian garden hermit. In the twenty-first century there is still a cultural memory of the ornamental hermit. This memory manifests itself in occasional advertisements for hermits, in the construction of modern hermitages, and in appearances of garden hermits in art, literature, and drama. Before turning to those subjects, we must attend to the problematical question of the extent to which the garden gnome might be seen as a cultural remnant of the garden hermit.

The garden gnome

The modern suburban garden, with its lawn, clipped hedges, flower beds, and water feature, was invented by the Dutch, and was a combination of French design and Dutch horticulture. The French influence was the *parterre* (French 'on the ground'), which was an ornamental garden laid out in geometrical designs; the outlines of the geometrical designs were formed with trimmed box, and the shapes were filled in with flower beds. The Dutch component was the planting: the Netherlands led Europe in horticultural botany, and suburban gardens were typically planted with tulips and hyacinths. As French gardens also made use of water, and the Netherlands had an abundance of canals, the water feature also became part of the suburban garden. The lawn had long been a feature of parks and gardens, and in suburban gardens sometimes consisted of camomile until the invention of the lawn mower enabled grass to be trimmed without recourse to scythes, scissors, or sheep.

In 1812, Johanna Schopenhauer (writer, *salonière*, and mother of the philosopher Arthur Schopenhauer) visited the Dutch village of Broek, in South Holland, and described the gardens that she saw in front of the houses. She noted the clipped trees and the architectural features carved from yew, and then turned to the statuary:

> In the middle of the garden stands the choicest decoration, perhaps a Dutch man sitting on a tub, and very highly coloured, or perhaps the figure of a Turk smoking his pipe, or an enormous flower-basket with the figure of a gardener looking out of it roguishly.

The human figure in the garden is not unprecedented, because in sixteenth-century France Bernard Palissy (potter, natural historian, and garden designer) had placed life-sized models of human figures on balconies overlooking the gardens that he designed; some of these figures were automatons, and so could move and emit sounds. But as the garden became smaller, so the figures became smaller. Figures are still present in twenty-first-century gardens. I have a 'circle of friends' based on Mayan figurines in my garden, and others have chosen smiling Buddhas or classical figures or children. Most popular of all, albeit only in certain social strata, is the garden gnome, which (unlike the ornamental hermit) has a huge following, a learned literature, and a considerable number of blogs and websites, some of which are dedicated to the liberation of gnomes who have been enslaved in gardens: there is one for the American Garden Gnome Liberation Front and another for the Front de Libération des Nains de Jardins. Such silliness may make the contention that the garden gnome is in any sense the successor to the ornamental hermit seem facile, but that is because the anodyne modern garden gnome has grown away from its origins in folklore, thanks in significant part to Walt Disney.

The garden gnome seems to have originated in the German state of Thuringia in the nineteenth century, but its antecedents are much older, reaching back to statues of dwarfs in the gardens of the Renaissance. In the Boboli gardens in Florence, for example, there is a full-sized statue (carved by Valerio Cioli in the 1560s) of a dwarf (Italian *gobbo*) nicknamed 'Morgante' at the court of Cosimo I de' Medici, portrayed as a drunken Bacchus riding on a tortoise. In 1621 Jacques Callot, a French etcher and engraver who spent much of his career in Italy, published a collection of designs for statues of *gobbi* entertainers. The collection proved to be influential, and soon statues based on Callot's designs began to appear in gardens all over northern Europe, especially in the German-speaking countries of the Holy Roman Empire. These statues, which were commonly known as callots, became popular in eighteenth-century German gardens.

The spiritual world of northern Europe was officially Protestant, but in practice there was widespread belief in ghosts and goblins, and these unofficial spiritual beings included the mythical 'little people' who worked underground. When these unseen creatures, ranging from Swedish *tomtar* to Danish *nissen*, Dutch *kabouter* and German *Zwergen*, were finally embodied in porcelain, they took the form of dwarfs, probably under the influence of Italian *gobbi*. In the late eighteenth century porcelain figures of dwarfs were manufactured in Germany, and then in England by Derby (later Crown Derby), but these figures were intended to be kept indoors.

In the German tradition the dwarfs were normally benign, as in the tale of 'Snow White and the Seven Dwarfs' collected by the Grimm brothers. In that version of the tale the dwarfs are miners, whereas in non-Germanic versions they are usually robbers. It may have been the tradition of dwarfs as good-natured miners that accounted for the triumph of the German garden gnome. It is possible that some porcelain figures were kept outdoors, but the first gnomes manufactured specifically for the garden appeared in Thuringia in the 1840s. Early garden gnomes already had the features of their modern descendants, including white beards, pointed red hats, and tools, though in the first instance the tools were related to mining rather than gardening. The traditional pointed hat is similar to the one worn by the Reverend Henry White in his capacity of ornamental hermit.

Several German manufacturers claim to have manufactured the first ceramic garden gnome, but the absence of evidence makes their rival claims hard to evaluate. What is clear, however, is that the most important centre for the manufacture of garden gnomes soon became the village of Gräfenroda, in Thuringia. At one point the village boasted sixteen manufacturers of gnomes, and although only one factory (Griebel) has survived into the twenty-first century, the village maintains its link with the tradition, and indeed has a museum of the history of garden gnomes.

The two best-known English collectors of German garden gnomes were Sir Charles Isham, whose gnomery was at Lamport Hall (Northamptonshire), and Sir Frank Crisp, who created a gnome garden for Friar Park (Oxfordshire). In 1846 Sir Charles Isham, the tenth baronet, inherited Lamport Hall, in which his family had lived since 1560, and immediately set about developing his estate by rebuilding cottages and improving the garden. The following year he embarked on his most enduring project, the construction of a large rockery in which he planted the first alpine garden in England. He built a high ironstone wall (which when seen from the lawn resembles the ruins of a country house), and behind it constructed the rockery, which he populated with gnomes. Belief in fairies and gnomes had declined in the course of the previous century, but Sir Charles was a firm believer in both, and thought that mines were inhabited by helpful gnomes who through sounds and lights led miners to the richest seams. On a visit to Nuremburg he found gnomes with mining equipment such as pick-axes and barrows, and brought them home for his rockery. His colony of gnomes was well established by the 1860s, which makes it the first in England. Unhappily, the colony has been dispersed, because after his death his elder surviving daughter, Louisa Corbett, ordered that the gnomes be removed. Fifty years later Sir Gyles Isham, the twelfth baronet, embarked on a restoration of the rockery, and discovered a gnome who had hidden in a crevice and so escaped the eviction ordered by Mrs Corbett. This gnome, which is said to be the earliest surviving garden gnome in England, now lives in the comfort of the house.

Friar Park, near Henley-on-Thames, is best known as the home of the former Beatle George Harrison, who, together with his wife

Olivia, restored the gardens. In the nineteenth century Friar Park was the country home of the lawyer, microscopist, and horticultural-ist Sir Frank Crisp, who used it as a setting for his lavish hospitality during the Henley Regatta, when he regularly entertained royalty. One part of his garden was a rockery of which the centrepiece was a replica of the Matterhorn (which had recently been climbed for the first time) more than six metres high, capped with a rock from the real Matterhorn. The rockery contained a series of underground chambers where his gnomes worked. The gnome collection was eventually dispersed, but the Harrisons managed to recover some of them in time for them to pose with George Harrison for the cover of 'All Things Must Pass'. Harrison also commemorated Sir Frank Crisp in 'The Ballad of Sir Frankie Crisp (Let it Roll)'. The interest of the Beatles in the Transcendental Meditation movement led by Mahari-shi Mahesh Yogi had its distant origins in the contemplative ideals associated with the garden hermit, and the image of George Harri-son posing with gnomes that represented the spirits of the under-ground recalls the Enlightenment ideal of man connected with nature.

These are the two best-known collections of gnomes, but there were many other nineteenth-century estates with resident gnomes. At the time gnomes were associated with upper-class gardens, but their social status has declined, and ceramics and terracotta have in large part been supplanted by plastic and resin. The turning point in the cultural fortunes of the garden gnome occurred in 1937, when Walt Disney transformed the gnomes from their traditional role (in Erasmus Darwin's phrase) as 'the guards and guides of Nature's chemic toil' into the cute figures of the animated *Snow White and the Seven Dwarfs*, giving them sentimental names (Bashful, Dopey, etc.).

Thereafter the gnome became a saccharine figure, and some people retreated in embarrassment. In 2008 the Chelsea Flower Show included a garden in memory of George Harrison, but no gnomes were included, because the Royal Horticultural Society bans gnomes from Chelsea, presumably because gnomes are *déclassé*; the following year a gnome successfully infiltrated a garden at the show, but was ejected before the judging began.

In literature the gnomes achieved their apotheosis in the series of gnome books (initially published in Dutch) written by Wil Huygen and illustrated by Rien Poortvliet. These books (*Gnomes, The Secret Book of Gnomes, Gnome Life, A Gnome Christmas*) were translated into many languages, and *The Secret Book of Gnomes* formed the basis of two Spanish cartoon series, *David el Gnomo* and *La llamada de los gnomos* ('the wisdom of the gnomes'). The most recent manifestation of gnomomania is *Gnomeo and Juliet*, a computer-animated feature film released in February 2011. In this version of Shakespeare's play, Capulets are represented as red gnomes and Montagues as blue gnomes. As an adaptation of *Romeo and Juliet*, this film may fall short of the standard achieved in Kenneth MacMillan's production of Prokofiev's ballet as danced by Rudolf Nureyev and Margot Fonteyn, but it does give gnomes a few minutes of flickering glory on the silver screen.

To what extent does the garden gnome continue the history of the ornamental hermit? The link is certainly not direct, in that gnomes have their own distinctive history, but there is a case for thinking of a succession in which gnomes came to occupy the cultural void occasioned by the demise of the ornamental hermit. The hermit and the gnome are both human figures in the garden, figures with historical and mythical resonances. The ornamental hermit has all but disappeared, whereas gnomes live on as distressed gentlefolk, banned from Chelsea but nonetheless indomitable in spirit. Indeed, there are signs of a come-back: the Gnome Reserve in Devon (where visitors are encouraged to wear red gnome hats) attracts tens of thousands of visitors every year, the BBC has introduced a character called Gordon the Garden Gnome (in honour, I presume, of authors with white beards called Gordon), and the Royal Botanic Gardens at Kew not only accommodates the Chief Gnome of the BBC cartoon in its false acacia, but also sells gnomes in its shop and uses Gordon the Garden Gnome leaflets to guide young visitors around the gardens. In the Lake District, Wast Water (England's deepest lake) is the home of a colony of gnomes whose numbers expand by immigration (new gnomes are left by visiting divers) rather than by natural reproduction.

The immense popularity of the Disney version of *Snow White* facilitated the creation of a modern garden gnome that is culturally bland and wholly unsupported by an underlying ideology, but the pre-Disney gnome represented a link with the natural world and so with earlier figures in the garden. It may not be altogether foolish to see a succession that extends from the living garden hermit to the stuffed hermit and the garden statue to the early garden gnomes collected by gentry families. By the time we arrive at *Gnomeo and Juliet*, the distant recollection of the garden hermit has been lost.

The contemporary hermit

Working as an ornamental hermit was always a specialist niche, and so it remains now, but in the twenty-first century three posts have been advertised and filled.

First, Painshill, for which the account in Chapter 4 carried the story up to the sale of the property in 1773. The estate then passed through a succession of owners, several of whom continued to develop the house and gardens. In World War II, however, Painshill was requisitioned for the Canadian Army, and in 1948 was acquired by the Baroness de Veauce, who converted the main house into apartments and the grounds into separate lots and then sold the estate piecemeal. Many of the original features of the garden survived this process, but decay was inevitable. In 1975 a group of Cobham residents joined forces with the Garden History Society and the Georgian Group, and began to acquire the land. By 1980, 153 acres (62 hectares) had been acquired, whereupon the Painshill Park Trust was established. The Trust has systematically restored many of the original features, including the Gothic temple, the ruined abbey, the Chinese bridge, the Turkish tent, the capacious grotto, the Gothic tower. The hermitage had been dismantled in the nineteenth century, leaving only the roughly shaped tree trunks; these in turn became firewood for the family living in the nearby Gothic tower, which meant that there was nothing to restore. The solution was a new hermitage in the image of the old one, and this was built on a remote wooded hill in 2004.

When the new hermitage was completed, two Lambeth organizations, the Danielle Arnaud Gallery and the Museum of Garden History, commissioned the performance artist David Blandy to serve for the first two weeks of June as the Painshill hermit. Health and Safety regulations meant that Blandy was not allowed to remain in the hermitage overnight, but in other ways he attempted to mimic the life of a hermit. He grew his hair long by way of preparation, and was barefoot throughout; the only contemporary aspect of his appearance

FIGURE **6.1** The new hermitage, Painshill.

was his decision to dress as a Buddhist Shaolin monk. Food and water were supplied by a costumed servant, but silence was maintained, at least in the sense that they did not speak. He did, however, listen to 1970s soul music. His purpose in assuming the role of the hermit was to demonstrate the loneliness of contemporary society, in which we spend much of our time in the seclusion of our homes.

In the same summer of 2002, Staffordshire County Council commissioned a project called 'Hidden Estates', in which artists worked at three Staffordshire estates. One of the estates was Shugborough, where the Council mounted an exhibition called 'Solitude'. In August the post of hermit-in-residence was advertised in *The Guardian, The London Review of Books, The Stage,* and the *Staffordshire Newsletter*:

> RESIDENT HERMIT required, for Week-End of 21ˢᵗ–22ⁿᵈ September, at Great Haywood Cliffs, formerly on SHUGBOROUGH ESTATE, in the County of Staffordshire; to PERFORM the Role of 'Resident Hermit': WILDERNESS & STIPEND provided.

The post was well paid (£600), and although a commodious cave was provided, Health and Safety regulations once again dictated that the hermit not be allowed to sleep in it, lest a killer rockfall render the solitude permanent. The hermit would be required to supply his or her own tent, and was allowed to bring a Swiss Army knife, a stool, chair, or blanket, a spiritual text, and another text concerning solitude. In marked contrast to the Painshill project, which abhorred the solitude of contemporary life, the Shugborough project was designed to celebrate solitude. The project manager explained that the idea was

> to enquire about the relevance and resonance of the concept of 'ornamental hermit' in a contemporary context, and to present the result of my enquiry in a work of art which combined elements from installation and performance, and involved the participation of a live individual. The project Solitude explores and contests the dread and contempt society now displays for the once fashionable ideal of solitude. Whilst, today, the wish for self improvement is rife; by contrast, the wish to be alone is not only unfashionable, but regarded as a sign of failure or unsociability.... Within what looks like a bit of fun, people will consider ideas that go back to Rousseau and Pope. It's a philosophical critique of the world in which we live. It's also an antidote to Big Brother reality television.

It may seem extraordinary that Staffordshire County Council chose to fund a programme that deprecated self-improvement as 'rife', but it is true that ornamental hermits are not necessarily self-improvers.

Reuters picked up the advertisement and syndicated it, so enquiries and applications came in from around the world. The successful candidate was Ansuman Biswas, an interdisciplinary performance artist whose CV includes directing, translating, designing underwater sculptures, touring with Björk, and travelling with shamans in the Gobi Desert. His most relevant experiences, however, were probably being sealed in a box for ten days and running seminars for Burmese monks. In the event, hundreds of people visited the cave in the course of the weekend. Children behaved themselves, but journalists had to be managed, so they were obliged to sit under a tree and meditate before being granted access to the hermit.

Ansuman Biswas was clearly deemed to be a successful hermit, because in August 2009 he was appointed to another hermitship, this time for a biblical forty days and nights in a Gothic tower above the Manchester Museum, which is the museum of the University of Manchester. The Museum announced that

> Through a Hermit's Blog, he hopes to engage members of the public in debate about why museums collect and preserve objects, whilst allowing species and cultures to become forgotten and extinct. He will also question the relationship of human beings to the natural world, hinting at the inevitable extinction of the human race itself. Confronted by facts about extinction, Biswas will respond by personally embodying this loss. He will become symbolically dead, renouncing his own liberty and cutting himself off from all physical contact.

And that is what happened. The curious viewer could follow the progress of the exhibition through a webcam (this was a thoroughly modern hermitage). As the blog developed, Mr Biswas came to reflect on what sort of hermit he was:

The hermit is conventionally a benign and pious figure, but I also want to invoke his destructive aspect. Artistic precedents for this approach are in the auto-destructive art of Gustav Metzger and John Latham. Eremetic forerunners include the great Hindu ascetic Shiva, who is celebrated as the destroyer of the world, and the Christian anchorite, Anthony the Great who burned away his wilfulness in order to surrender himself to the will of God. My own hermetic training is in the Theravada Buddhist technique of Vipassana [which] is essentially an exhaustive cataloguing of every aspect of experience, up to and including the cessation of everything.

The hermit has become a figure who has transcended melancholy in favour of a destructive or auto-destructive art. This movement originated when Gustav Metzger began to spray acid onto sheets of nylon as a symbolic protest against nuclear weapons; the idea was that the nylon writhed as it changed shape, and so was auto-creative and auto-destructive. In a similar vein, John Latham built three piles of books (called 'the Laws of England') on the pavement in front of the British Museum, and set them alight. In such acts the principled solitude of the hermit has been displaced by principled destruction, and so Mr Biswas announced that he proposed to destroy the objects that he had selected from the museum's collection. In the event, there was little enthusiasm for this course of action.

The contemporary hermitage

In recent years the hermitage has enjoyed a minor renaissance. One of the finest contemporary hermitages is in St Fiachra's Garden, which is located at the Irish National Stud (Tully, County Kildare). Fiacre (the English spelling of Irish Fiachra) was a sixth-century Irish hermit who travelled to Meaux (north-east of Paris), where the bishop gave him land on which to build a hermitage in what is now the village of Saint-Fiacre (formerly Brogillum, later Breuil). His name has become the French word for taxi (*fiacre*), because the Hôtel de St-Fiacre (Rue St-Martin, Paris) named after him has had carriages for hire since the seventeenth century; for this reason he is the patron saint of taxi drivers. Fiacre's hermitage had sufficient land for him to plant a garden, and he became well known for his medicinal herbs. Fiacre's skill in horticulture led to his becoming the patron saint of gardeners, and it is in this capacity that he is honoured at the National Stud, where St Fiachra's Garden was opened in 1999 to celebrate the Millennium.

The garden is on a four-acre (1.6 hectare) woodland site with several small lakes. Entry to the garden is through an underground stone passage, just like the eighteenth-century hermitage at the Falls of Acharn. A woodland walk leads to a hermitage on the side of a lake. A life-sized statue of the saint is seated on a rocky peninsula; he holds a seed in his hand. The hermitage has two cells, loosely modelled on the magnificent (but difficult of access) stone 'beehive' huts (clocháns) at the monastic complex on Sceilig Mhichíl (Skellig Michael), 13 kilometres off the coast of County Kerry. The larger of the two cells has in its floor a delicate subterranean garden of rocks, ferns, fossils, and orchids, all hand crafted by Waterford Crystal. This hermitage is not an archaeological reconstruction, and has not been conceived in an antiquarian spirit, but is rather an attempt to evoke in a garden setting the monastic movement in sixth- and seventh-century Ireland. There is no evocation of the hardship suffered by the monks of Sceilig Mhichíl, or of the hermit (whose hut is lost) on the island's South Peak, but the spiritual peace of the recluse is admirably captured in the tranquility of the setting of this remarkable modern hermitage.

FIGURE 6.2 St Fiachra's hermitage, Irish National Stud.

In England there is a growing number of new hermitages, such as the small thatched hermitage, possibly from a Wright design, at Hampton Court Castle, in Herefordshire (not to be confused with Hampton Court Palace). This is a simple shelter by a waterfall, and well integrated into its constructed landscape. Of the new hermitages of which I am aware, the finest example is the one in the Wilderness Garden at Elton Hall, the home (straddling the Cambridgeshire–Northamptonshire border) of Sir William and Lady Proby. Sir William is a former president of the Historic Houses Association and a former chairman of the National Trust, and as his mind is furnished with a deep knowledge of landscape and architecture, his wife commissioned the hermitage as a surprise for his fiftieth birthday. On the day he was presented with a model of the building, which was constructed in 1999 by Raffles Garden Buildings. Sir William's hermitage is, unsurprisingly, a carefully meditated revival. The designer, David Raffle, has described it:

The floor was cobbled from roundels of cedar and pine to create an aromatic atmosphere. Amongst these pale colours darker yew was introduced to create a MW pattern for William & Meredyth.... Corsican pine slab wood was selected to form the walls, leaving an open arch for the door and gothic arches cut from huge slabs of pine. The same tree was used to form the table and chairs from a design found at Brocklesby Park Hermitage. The rafters came from Shropshire Marches, joined by a boss at the apex of the roof, which was cloaked, with a chestnut burr grown at Florence Court [County Fermanagh], which had grown against a 'Thomas Wright' Heather House. The zigzag hazel laths continue the M and W theme and support the traditional wheat straw thatch surmounted by a Yew Cross. Above the fireplace is the rhyme,

> 'Through cunning with dibble,
> rake, mattock and spade,
> by line and by level,
> trim garden is made.'
> Thomas Tusser 1557.

At the rear of the structure a small alcove together with its shuttered, leaded lights, forms the bed. On the underside of the alcove roof it is decorated with signs of the Zodiac [representing the star signs of all the family] and will have drapes and cushions, perhaps deviating from the solitude of the hermit's life but adding to the romance of the building.

In the event, the drapes and cushions were never added, and the bare wood hints at the austerity of the imagined hermit's life. The overall effect of the building is enhanced by its setting: on entering the wilderness, which was laid out by Lady Proby some 30 years ago, the visitor sees the hermitage at the end of a broad walk, and there are fine views along radial paths from the hermitage.

In addition to these modern hermitages, there are also recent examples of rootwork, which had its origins in the garden hermitage. The architectural historian Gervase Jackson-Stops used rootwork in a temple in the gardens of Horton Menagerie, Northamptonshire

FIGURE **6.3** The hermitage, Elton Hall.

(designed by Thomas Wright), and the garden designer Julian Ban-
nerman incorporated rootwork into his innovative grotto at Leeds
Castle, in Kent. These are not hermitages, but they constitute evidence for the cultural memory of the hermitage in the architectural
imagination.

The hermit in the imagination

The ornamental hermit lives on in the visual, literary, and dramatic
imagination. In painting, the best recent example is *An Ornamental
Hermit* (2007) (see Plate 11), by the Welsh artist Geraint Evans

which was one of the winners of the 'John Moores 25' exhibition, and was hung at the Walker Art Gallery in Liverpool in 2008–9. The painting shows a suburban family posing in their garden, as if for a photograph. In the background is a tree-house, which is the home of the hermit who stands with the family. The artist has a particular interest in the suburban garden and in what he describes as 'the simulated and constructed landscapes that are often found within the city and that offer safe and yet possibly aspirational encounters with "authentic", uncultivated nature'. In this painting he transplants the ornamental hermit of the eighteenth-century picturesque garden into the suburban garden of the twenty-first century. The artful rusticity of the tree-house and the bizarre image of the half-naked hermit represent gestures towards Rousseau's notion of the natural world. The painting is a good-humoured depiction of the absurdity of emblematic rusticity.

The hermit also appears in twentieth-century literature. One example is *Stop Press* (1939), a crime novel by 'Michael Innes' (the pseudonym of J. I. M. Stewart) in the Inspector Appleby series. In this novel, a character called Jasper Scoon builds a 'dream-Gothic' pile called Scoon Abbey, which is surrounded by 'the Gardens of Idea—gloomy groves, murmuring streams, sequestered grots, root-houses, urns, dells, denes, dingles'. Scoon warns his guests at the Abbey not to approach the hermit, who is bad-tempered, and seems not to have a vocation for the contemplative life. Scoon, he explains, had tried to assist the hermit, because 'a hermit on an estate should always be regarded as the direct responsibility of the owner'. Matters had come to a head when the hermit complained that his cell was damp. Scoon acknowledged that this was the case ('one could hardly have a hermit's cell constructed in any other way') but was loath to dismiss the hermit: 'consider the position of an unsuccessful hermit out of employment. The openings are very few.' Scoon therefore decided to allow the hermit to move to a nearby cellarium, but acknowledged that he was now a hermit in no more than name: ' "Alas!", said Shoon, "I fear he is only *acting* the part".' In the event, this turns out to be truer than the reader imagines: the real purpose of the hermit's move is to guard the cellarium, which is a weapons cache.

Mick Jackson's 'Hermit Wanted', in *Ten Sorry Tales* (2006), which has twice been memorably read on radio (by Penelope Wilton and Prunella Scales) begins as a story about a wealthy couple called Giles and Virginia Jarvis, who decide to engage a hermit to live in a cave that they have found on their estate. Like Jasper Scoon's hermit, the Jarvis hermit turns out not to be what he seems, and the story soon darkens in a manner reminiscent of Roald Dahl's short stories for adults. 'Hermit Wanted' is a powerful story, but not for the faint-hearted. In America, Alison Lurie's *Foreign Affairs* (which won the Pulitzer Prize) includes a character trying to track down a lordly ancestor who retreated to a cave on his estate to live as a hermit.

In poetry, the finest modern poem on the subject of the hermit is Seamus Heaney's 'The Hermit', in *Station Island* (1984), whom the poet observed

> As he prowled the rim of his clearing
> where the blade of choice had not spared
> one stump of affection...

This affirmation of the 'work of refreshment', in the tradition of Virgil's *Georgics*, is a powerful statement of the restorative effects of solitary labour. On the hermit in the garden, there is a fine poem entitled 'The Ornamental Hermit' by Matthew Francis, in *Dragons* (2001); the poem, which won the *TLS*/Blackwells poetry competition in 2000, insightfully portrays the hermit as the affective link between the landowner and the landscape.

It is time to conclude this study by attending to a comic but intellectually serious contemporary treatment of the role of the ornamental hermit in understanding the prospect of the eventual extinction of the human race.

The garden hermit evolved from the antiquarian druid and eventually declined into the garden gnome. His final apotheosis was achieved in Tom Stoppard's *Arcadia*, which has been acclaimed as the greatest drama of ideas of the late twentieth century and proposed by one critic (writing for *The Independent*) as 'perhaps the greatest play of its time'. The first production, directed by Trevor Nunn, opened in April 1993 at the National Theatre in London. Two years later Trevor Nunn took the play to New York, where it was performed with a wholly new cast at the Vivian Beaumont Theater at the Lincoln Center. The play was revived at the Duke of York's Theatre (London) in 2009 and at the Ethel Barrymore Theatre (New York) in 2011.

The play is set in Sidley Park, a fictional country house in Derbyshire; it alternates between the late Georgian period (1809–12) and the present, with two sets of characters who occupy a single set. The principal characters in the Georgian scenes are a tutor, Septimus Hodge, and the daughter of the house (Hodge's pupil), Thomasina Coverly; these characters are loosely modelled on Eduard and Ottilie, the protagonists of Goethe's *Die Wahlverwandtschaften* (*Elective Affinities*), which was published in 1809, the year in which *Arcadia* opens. In the scenes representing the present in *Arcadia*, two investigators gradually uncover the events of 1809–12. One is a writer called Hannah Jarvis, who is seeking information about a hermit who once lived in the garden, and the other is an academic called Bernard Nightingale, who is investigating an incident in the life of Byron.

In the first of the play's seven scenes (in two acts), Thomasina, who is a mathematical prodigy, contemplates the notion of determinism, prompted by the question of why jam stirred into rice pudding can never be unstirred. A landscape architect enters with two other characters, and they discuss a new design for the gardens of Sidley. The picture of the garden that the architect presents includes a hermitage, and Thomasina adds an image of a hermit, drawn to resemble John the Baptist. In scene 4 Hannah discovers the notebook of Thomasina containing speculations on chaos theory and algorithmic iteration, and in scene 5 (Act 2 scene 1) Hannah begins to hypothesize that the hermit may have been Septimus. In the final scene past and present are brought together. Thomasina explains the concept of entropy, which shows that the universe is winding down, and characters from past and present examine a diagram that Thomasina has drawn to demonstrate the irreversibility of heat (an anticipation of the second law of thermodynamics), which means that at the end of time everything will be at room temperature. Thomasina dies that night in a fire, and the hermit assumes the task of using algebra to evaluate Thomasina's overturning of Newtonian physics. It is implied, but not stated explicitly, that it was Septimus who became the hermit, and devoted the rest of his life to this task. A play that began as a country house farce ends with a garden hermit's protracted consideration of the mathematics of the death of the universe.

Stoppard uses the changing fashion in garden design to illustrate a broader cultural movement from the Enlightenment to Romanticism, a shift that Hannah memorably describes as 'a decline from thinking to feeling'. Lady Croom (Thomasina's mother) explains this decline in terms of garden history: 'the familiar pastoral refinement of an Englishman's garden [will be replaced by] an eruption of gloomy forest and towering crag, of ruins where there was never a house, of water dashing against rocks where there was never a spring. My hyacinth dell is to become a haunt for hobgoblins.' An Arcadian paradise becomes a chaotic romantic landscape, and a hermit is inserted into this landscape. Lady Croom demands that a hermit be found to occupy the ornamental hermitage, arguing that 'if I am promised a fountain I expect it to come with water'. The designer suggests advertising for a hermit in the newspaper, and she replies, 'but surely a hermit who takes a newspaper is not a hermit in whom one can have complete confidence'.

Arcadia is a play that (in the words of *Love's Labour's Lost*) 'move[s] wild laughter in the throat of death'. The science anticipated by Thomasina renders inevitable the death of the individual, the species, and the known universe. The loss of certainty in the shift from classical garden design to romantic, picturesque design is paralleled in science by the shift from stable Newtonian physics to unstable chaos that will end in annihilation. How best, Stoppard wonders, can we live with that knowledge? The answer lies in the endeavours of the hermit to understand. As Hannah explains to Valentine,

It's wanting to know that makes us matter. That's why you can't believe in the afterlife, Valentine. Believe in the after, by all means, but not the life. Believe in God, the soul, the spirit, believe in angels if you like, but not in the great celestial get-together for an exchange of views. If the answers are in the back of the book I can wait, but what a drag. Better to struggle on knowing that failure is final.

The play ends with a dance of death, a waltz in which the classical merges with the romantic and the past with the present as the final conflagration adumbrated in the house-fire draws ever nearer. The struggle to understand embodied in the hermit in the garden may seem futile, but it is that struggle that enables the individual to carry on knowing, as Hannah says, that failure is final. The vision of human life enacted in this play, at once melancholic and risible, is a wondrous reworking of the eighteenth-century idea of the hermit in the garden.

The idea of a real or imagined hermit in a Georgian garden seems preposterous from the perspective of the twenty-first century, but did not seem silly to those who erected hermitages and employed hermits or pretended to be hermits or entered into the fiction that the hermit had just stepped out for a moment. Stoppard's *Arcadia* is the greatest articulation of the view that the forces that created the ornamental hermit are still at work.

A CATALOGUE OF HERMITAGES

This list records hermitages mentioned in this book, both religious and secular, including court hermitages; counties and countries are modern, not historical. Extant often means 'ruinous'.

Name	County	Present State
ENGLAND		
Ansley Park	Warwickshire	destroyed
Atherton Hall	Lancashire	destroyed
Badminton	Gloucestershire	extant
Barrells	Warwickshire	destroyed
Barrow House	Cumbria	destroyed
Bath (Lilliput Castle)	Somerset	destroyed
Bathampton	Somerset	destroyed
Bicton	Devon	extant
Birchover	Derbyshire	extant
Birmingham (Soho)	West Midlands	destroyed; replica built 2004
Borrowdale	Cumbria	destroyed
Bremhill	Wiltshire	destroyed
Bridgnorth	Shropshire	extant
Brocklesby	Lincolnshire	extant
Burley on the Hill	Rutland	destroyed
Cadland Manor	Hampshire	never built

Name	County	Present State
Carshalton House	Surrey	extant
Charterhouse	West Sussex	extant
Conishead Priory	Lancashire	destroyed
Dale Abbey	Derbyshire	extant
Dinton Hall	Buckinghamshire	extant
Downton Castle	Herefordshire	extant
Eastbourne	East Sussex	extant
Elton Hall	Cambridgeshire	new
Enstone	Oxfordshire	destroyed
Falling Foss	North Yorkshire	extant
Fonthill Abbey	Wiltshire	destroyed
Foremark	Derbyshire	extant
Frogmore	Berkshire	destroyed
Goodwood	West Sussex	extant
Grantham	Lincolnshire	destroyed
Hagley Park	Worcestershire	destroyed
Hampton Court Castle	Herefordshire	new
Hawkstone	Shropshire	destroyed 2008, replica built 2009
Kedleston	Derbyshire	extant
Killerton	Devon	extant
Lambeth	Greater London	destroyed
Leasowes, The	West Midlands	destroyed
Leeds (Roundhay)	West Yorkshire	destroyed
Lincoln's Inn Fields	London	extant
Lundy	Devon	destroyed
Marston House	Somerset	destroyed
Medmenham	Buckinghamshire	extant
Mereworth	Kent	destroyed
Midford Castle	Somerset	extant

Mount Grace Priory	North Yorkshire	twenty destroyed, one restored
Oldstone	Devon	extant
Olney	Buckinghamshire	destroyed
Oxton	Devon	destroyed
Painshill	Surrey	destroyed; replica built 2004
Percy Lodge	Buckinghamshire	destroyed
Rawdon	West Yorkshire	destroyed
Richmond	Surrey	destroyed
Salcombe Regis	Devon	extant
Selborne	Hampshire	two, both destroyed
Shugborough	Staffordshire	new
Sidley Park	Derbyshire	fictional
Southstone Rock	Worcestershire	extant
Spetchley Park	Worcestershire	extant
Stamford	Cambridgeshire	two, both destroyed
Stourhead	Wiltshire	destroyed
Stourport-on-Severn	Worcestershire	extant
Stowe	Buckinghamshire	extant
Tong	Shropshire	destroyed
Twickenham	Greater London	extant
Vauxhall Gardens	Greater London	destroyed
Virginia Water	Berkshire	destroyed or never built
Ware Park	Hertfordshire	extant
Warkworth	Northumbria	extant
Whitley	Essex	destroyed
Woodhouse	Staffordshire	destroyed
Wolverley	Worcestershire	extant
Wrest	Bedfordshire	destroyed

Name	County	Present State
IRELAND		
Belle Isle	Fermanagh	destroyed
Caledon	Tyrone	destroyed
Delville	Dublin	destroyed
Dundalk	Louth	destroyed
Florence Court	Fermanagh	destroyed, replica built 1993
Glin Castle	Limerick	extant
Greenmount	Antrim	extant
Innisfallen Island	Kerry	destroyed
Kilronan	Roscommon	extant
Loughgall	Armagh	extant
Luttrellstown	Dublin	destroyed
Marino House	Dublin	destroyed
Oriel Temple	Louth	extant
St Enda	Dublin	extant
St Fiacra	Kildare	new
Tollymore	Down	one destroyed, one extant
Waterstown	Westmeath	extant
ISLE OF MAN		
Calf of Man	Crown dependency	destroyed
SCOTLAND		
Acharn	Perthshire	extant
Craigieburn	Dumfriesshire	extant
Dalkeith	Midlothian	extant
Dunkeld	Perthshire	extant
Friars Carse	Dumfriesshire	extant
Hamilton Palace	Lanarkshire	destroyed
Kenmore	Perthshire	extant

The Continent	Country	Present State
Adelsnäs	Sweden	extant
Alameda de Osuna	Spain	destroyed
Aranjuez	Spain	thirteen, all destroyed
Arlesheim	Switzerland	extant
Bayreuth	Germany	extant
Beeckestijn	Netherlands	destroyed
Bonţida	Romania	destroyed
Budapest	Hungary	destroyed
Buen Retiro	Spain	five destroyed, two extant
Cetinale, Villa	Italy	extant
Chantilly	France	destroyed
Cleve	Germany	extant
Csákvár	Hungary	destroyed
Ermenonville	France	destroyed
Fagervik	Finland	extant
Forsmarks Bruk	Sweden	extant
Franchard	France	destroyed
Gaillon	France	two, both destroyed
Kuks	Czech Republic	five, all destroyed
Kuskova	Russia	extant
Laberinto de Horta, El	Spain	destroyed
Lerma	Spain	six destroyed, one extant
Louisenlund	Germany	extant
Marly	France	destroyed
Montserrat	Spain	five destroyed, two extant
Munich	Germany	extant
Nagycenk	Hungary	extant
Peterhof	Russia	extant
Potsdam	Germany	extant

The Continent	Country	Present State
Pushkin	Russia	extant
St Petersburg	Russia	extant
Sieglitzer Berg	Germany	destroyed
Vieil-Hesdin	France	destroyed
Weimar	Germany	extant
Wilhelmshöhe	Germany	extant
Wörlitz	Germany	extant
Yuste	Spain	extant
Zwernitz Castle	Germany	extant

THE HERMIT AND THE HERMITAGE
ON THE CONTINENT

I n the late eighteenth century the English landscape garden became fashionable on the Continent, where it was variously known as the *jardin anglais*,
the *giardino inglese*, and the *Englischer Garten*. Some of these gardens had ornamental hermitages. This brief survey will begin with Germany, where the influence of the English garden was first felt, and then turn to the Netherlands,
Scandinavia, Hungary (including Transylvania), Russia, Spain, and Switzerland.

The Continental country with the greatest number of hermitages in 'English'
gardens is Germany. Before the English style arrived, there was a fashion for
court hermitages, such as the Eremitage just outside Bayreuth and the slightly
later Schloss Nymphenburg, the summer residence of the Bavarian electors in
Munich. The original garden at Schloss Nymphenburg was Italianate, but in the
early eighteenth century the landscape architect Joseph Effner began to remodel
it. His principal contribution to the park at Nymphenburg was the erection of
three pavilions (the fourth and finest is the work of another architect, François
de Cuvilliés). One of Effner's pavilions was the Magdalenenklause (1725–8), a
hermitage constructed as a ruined cell. This was a structure that anticipated the
arrival of the English landscape style, which first appeared at Wörlitz, in Saxony-
Anhalt, eastern Germany.

The large garden at Wörlitz was created between 1764 and 1805 as part of
Schloss Wörlitz, the summer residence of Francis, Prince of Anhalt-Dessau.
Prince Francis was the ruler of Dessau, but he was also a garden designer of considerable distinction. He had travelled in England, and was familiar with English
gardens such as Kew, The Leasowes, Stowe, and Stourhead, all of which he drew

on when designing gardens at Luisium (1774), Sieglitzer Berg (1777), and Wörlitz. His garden at Wörlitz was designed in the spirit of Rousseau's Ermenonville, from which he took the use of poplars; indeed, in 1782 he installed a replica of Rousseau's tomb. On a distant part of the estate a small hermitage was built. Prince Francis's other gardens were not as elaborate, but he commissioned the German garden designer Johann Friedrich Eyserbeck to built a hermitage at Sieglitzer Berg, on the bank of the Elbe; the design clearly draws on Stourhead.

Visitors to Wörlitz included Duke Charles Augustus of Saxe-Weimar, who was accompanied by Goethe. On returning to Weimar they replicated some of its features in what is now called Ilm Park, which was laid out along the river. The buildings that they constructed in the park include a hermitage that is now called the Borkenhäuschen ('bark house'), which was built in 1778.

Two other English gardens in Germany have surviving hermitages, one in Kassel and the other in Potsdam. The castle and park at Kassel, known as Wilhelmshöhe since 1798, was laid out in the early eighteenth century as an Italian garden, with abundant use of water and a plethora of statues. In the early 1780s the Landgrave created a 'Chinese' village of Mulang in the park, so initiating the shift within the garden from an Italian baroque design to an English landscape garden. The buildings of Mulang were soon supplemented with an Egyptian pyramid, a temple of Mercury, and a group of wooden hermitages, each dedicated to a philosopher; only the Hermitage of Socrates survives.

The Neuer Garten in Potsdam was the creation of Frederick William [Friedrich Wilhelm] II, King of Prussia, who soon after his accession in 1786 commissioned Johann August Eyserbeck (son of Johann Friedrich) to implement his plans for a garden on the English model. At the north end of the park there is a hermitage, now crumbling, which had a reed roof, and was clad with oak bark.

The present border between Germany and the Netherlands is a relatively modern one. During the Thirty Years War the city of Cleve, which is now on the German side of the Dutch–German border, was controlled by the Dutch Republic.

When the War was concluded in 1647, the German elector of Brandenburg appointed the Dutch statesman Johan Maurits, Count of Nassau-Siegen, as stadholder of the duchy of Cleve, substantial parts of which were occupied by the Dutch. The seat of the duchy was Cleve, and the Count embarked on a large-scale redesign of the city. He rebuilt Schloss Schwanenburg (the official residence of the stadholder), commissioned a star-shaped network of roads, and created a series of landscaped parks. The last of these commissions was in Bedburg-Hau (5 km south-east of Cleve), where the Count commissioned his tomb at the side of the road (in Roman fashion) and retired from office to spend his last days in a hermitage, just as the Emperor Charles V had done.

The other Dutch garden hermitage was built at Beeckestijn, near Haarlem. In about 1764 Johann Georg Michael, who was responsible for the advent of the English landscape garden in the Netherlands, extended the formal garden of the Amsterdam merchant Jacob Boreel with a pioneering landscape garden. Buildings and follies in the Beeckestijn garden included a Corinthian arch, a gardener's cottage in the style of a Gothic chapel, and the first ornamental hermitage in the Netherlands. The landscape gardens created by Michael and his son-in-law Jan David Zocher the elder inaugurated a tradition that extended well into the twentieth century, so it is likely that a number of later gardens were also furnished with hermitages.

There are at least four English gardens in Scandinavia with hermitages. Fagervik, in the Finnish region of Uusimaa, is an eighteenth-century architectural survival, the work of Christian Fredrik Schröder, the town architect of Turku. In Fagervik he designed the manor house, a street of houses for blacksmiths, and an English landscape garden with a church, a Chinese pavilion (the only one in Finland) on a rock in the lake, and a hermitage.

Louisenlund is now in Germany, but in the eighteenth century it was the summer residence of the Danish governor of Schleswig-Holstein, the Landgrave Carl von Hessen. The garden is named after the Landgrave's consort, Princess Louise of Denmark and Norway (and daughter of King Frederick V of Denmark). The garden is Masonic in inspiration, and its symbols are not all understood. Its buildings include a Freimaurerturm ('tower of Freemasonry') and a hermitage with an Irrgarten ('labyrinth'). Friars Carse, in Scotland, had Masonic symbols added when it was restored, but Louisenlund seems to be the only instance of the design of a hermitage reflecting the ideas of Freemasonry.

There are also two hermitages in Sweden. Forsmarks Bruk, in Uppland, is a surviving eighteenth-century mill village, built as an ideal community. The manor house has a French garden on one side and an English landscape garden on the other. The English garden, which was built in the late 1780s, contains both a hermitage and a bark temple. Sweden's other hermitage is a twentieth-century creation by Rudolf Abelin, who often worked in historic styles. At Adelsnäs, on an isthmus in Lake Bysjön, in Östergötland (East Gothland), an English garden was laid out in the early nineteenth century; in the early twentieth century various arts-and-crafts buildings were erected, together with a hermitage designed by Abelin.

The ancient gardens of the royal castle at Buda (now incorporated into Budapest) have twice been destroyed: the Renaissance garden disappeared in the Siege of Buda in 1686, and the magnificent landscape garden that evolved in the centuries to follow was obliterated by bombing in World War II; the site is now a public park. The origins of the landscape garden lay in a design of 1765–6 by the Austrian architect Franz Anton Hillebrandt and the Dutch garden designer Adriaen van Steckhoven. In the 1790s this garden was extended beyond the castle walls; in this new section the buildings included a Gothic Dutch peasant's house and a hermitage—the only royal hermitage in Austro-Hungary.

The Esterházy were for centuries the most prominent family of statesmen in Austro-Hungary. Count János Esterházy, a member of the Tata branch of the family, decided in 1777 to make Csákvár the centre of his estates. Karl Ritter von Moreau, the French architect of the Esterházy family, was charged with remodelling the house; his responsibilities also included the creation of an English garden. Working with the stage designer Pietro Rivetti, he constructed an abundance of buildings in a variety of styles: houses in Dutch, Egyptian, and Chinese styles, a *hameau*, and a hermitage. The hermitage may have been inhabited by an estate worker responsible for the garden. That seems to have been the case at

Nagycenk, the seat of the Széchenyi family, where the occupant of the hermitage (which survives) had to work as a gardener and to ring the chapel bell.

For a millennium until 1918, Hungary included Transylvania (now in Romania). In Transylvania, the Bánffy family owned an estate at the village of Bonțida (Hungarian Bonchida, German Bonisbruck), near what is now Cluj-Napoca (Hungarian Kolozsvár, German Klausenburg). The geometrical eighteenth-century garden by Johann Christian Erras drew on Versailles and Schönbrunn, and during this period the estate became known as the Versailles of Transylvania. In the 1830s, however, this garden was replaced by Count József Bánffy with an English landscape garden designed by Sámuel Hermann and his successor János László. It was Hermann who was responsible for the garden buildings, which included temples, pavilions, a rustic fisherman's hut, and a hermitage. Both castle and garden were ruined during the German retreat of 1944, and the derelict estate was returned to the Bánffy family after the fall of communism. The castle is now the subject of a major restoration project by the Transylvania Trust, and the park is being restored by a Romanian trust called Pro Patrimonio.

Kuskova is a palace on the south-east edge of Moscow; it was the home of the Sheremet'yev family for more than 300 years, and since the revolution of 1917 has been the State Museum of Ceramics. In the mid-eighteenth century Count Pyotr Sheremet'yev commissioned the gardens that still exist today. Garden buildings include a stepped 'Dutch House' (1749–51), an 'Italian House' (1754–5), a grotto (1755–75), and a hermitage (1765–7). The hermitage was a collaboration between a serf architect and Karl Blank, a Russian architect of Huguenot descent. It is a circular pavilion with graceful proportions, situated at the convergence of eight paths. The Count used it as a personal retreat, choosing to spend much of his time in the hermitage rather than the palace. Other buildings in the park have disappeared, but the hermitage still remains.

In Spain, there were two important English landscape gardens. El Laberinto de Horta (1794), near Barcelona, was designed by the Italian Domenico Bagutti, who furnished it with its famous cypress maze (still in immaculate condition) as well as temples, statues, a grotto, and (in a shady corner) a hermitage. The Alameda de Osuna, the garden of the Palacio El Capricho, on the edge of Madrid, was the Rousseauesque creation of the Duquesa de Osuna (wife of the ninth Duque). Garden buildings constructed in the early 1790s included a rustic house (La casa de la vieja) and a hermitage; both were the work of the Italian painter and stage designer Angel Maria Tadey. The hermitage, like a stage set, achieved the illusion of dilapidation by the skilful use of paint: the cracks in the walls, for example, are painted rather than real, as is the moss. It is said that a religious hermit called Brother Arsenio lived in the hermitage for 26 years until his death in 1802, that he was succeeded by his friend Brother Eusebio, and that in 1816 living hermits were replaced by an automaton. Perhaps this is so, in which case these would be the last garden hermits in Spain. Evidence for this contention exists in the form of religious paintings beneath the *trompe-l'œil* dilapidation. It seems equally likely that these hermits were fictions, just like the temporarily absent hermits in English gardens in Britain and Ireland; evidence for this view is the confused chronology of Brother Arsenio, who seems to have lived in the hermitage many years before it was built.

The largest and finest English landscape garden in Switzerland is the Ermitage at Arlesheim, some 10 km south-east of Basel. The garden was established in 1785 as an attempt to realize the ideals of Rousseau as articulated in *La nouvelle Héloïse*. The garden was destroyed by French troops in 1793, but restored in the early nineteenth century (1810–12), when new monuments and follies (notably grottoes) were added. From the outset there was a playground and a carousel to facilitate the process whereby children could enjoy themselves while learning from nature. At the centre of the park a root-house clad in bark accommodated a hermit. The first hermit was a wooden statue, but he was soon replaced by a wooden automaton who nodded sagely when visitors arrived and then went back to reading his book. The current hermit has a begging bowl, and nods his head in thanks when coins are placed in the bowl by visitors (see Plate 12). He is Europe's last surviving ornamental hermit.

WORKS CONSULTED

Grove Dictionary of Art/Grove Art Online

Adam, Robert (1728–92)

Amboise, Cardinal Georges d' (1460–1510)

Anhalt-Dessau, (Leopold III Frederick) Francis, Prince of [Anhalt, Duke of] (1740–1817)

Apollodorus of Damascus (d. *c.* AD 125)

Aranjuez Palace

Batoni, Pompeo (1708–87)

Boulton, Matthew (1728–1809)

Braun, Matyáš Bernard (1684–1738)

Bridgeman, Charles (d. 1738)

Brown, (Lancelot) 'Capability' (1716–83)

Buda Castle (s.v. Budapest IV. Buda Castle)

Callot, Jacques (1592–1635)

Campbell, Colen (1676–1729)

Caprarola, Villa [Palazzo] Farnese

Carter, John (1748–1817)

Castle, Richard (?1690–1751)

Catherine II [Catherine the Great], Empress of Russia [Sophie Friederike Auguste von Anhalt-Zerbst] (1729–96), (s.v. Romanov (3))

Chambers, Sir William (1723–96)

Chantilly, Château de

Charles V, Holy Roman Emperor (1500–58) (s.v. Habsburg, §I (5))

Charles Augustus [Carl August; Karl August], Duke (from 1815 Grand Duke) of Saxe-Weimar (1757–1828) (s.v. Wettin, House of (11))

Chigi, Fabio, Pope Alexander VII (1599–1667)

Chigi, Flavio (1631–93)

Cioli, Valerio (1529–99)

Crescenzi, Giovanni Battista (1577–1635)

Dezallier d'Argenville, Antoine-Nicolas (1723–96)

Du Cerceau, Jacques Androuet (c.1515–85)

Effner, Joseph (1687–1745)

Elizabeth, Empress of Russia (1709–62) (s.v. Romanov (2))

Ermenonville

Escorial

Esterházy

Evelyn, John (1620–1706)

Folly

Fontana, Carlo (1638–1714)

Frederick William [Friedrich Wilhelm] II, King of Prussia (1744–97)
  (s.v. Hohenzollern (9))

Gaillon, Château de

Gazebo

Ghiberti, Lorenzo di Cione (1378–1455)

Gillespie Graham, James (1776–1855)

Gilpin, William (1724–1804)

Girardin, Louis-René, Marquis de (1735–1808)

Grotto

Guelfi, Giovanni Battista (fl. 1714–34)

Hadrian's Villa (s.v. Tivoli 2 (i))

Hermitage

Herrera Barnuevo, Antonio de (fl. 1621; d. 1646)

Hill, David Octavius (1802–70) (s.v. Hill and Adamson)

Hillebrandt, Franz Anton (1719–91)

Hoare, Henry the younger (1705–85)

Hoare, Sir (Richard) Colt, second baronet (1758–1838)

Jefferson, Thomas (1743–1826)

Keene, Henry (1726–76)

Kent, William (1686–1748)

Kew, Royal Botanic Gardens of

Knight, Richard Payne (1751–1824)

Kuks

Kuskovo

Langley, Batty (1696–1751)

Leasowes, The

Lely, Sir Peter (1618–80)

Le Nôtre, André (1613–1700)

Lens, Bernard III (1681–1740) (s.v. Lens)

Lerma

Ligorio, Pirro (c.1513–83)

Marie-Antoinette (-Josèphe-Jeanne), Queen of France (1755–93) (s.v. Bourbon, §I (12))

Maurits, Johan, Count of Nassau-Siegen (1604–79) (s.v. Nassau (1))

Medici, Cosimo I de (1519–74) (s.v. Medici, de' (14))

Miller, Sanderson (1716–80)

Mique, Richard (1724–94)

Monticello

Mora, Francisco de (1552–1610)

Moreau, Karl, Ritter von (?1758–1840)

Morris, Roger (1695–1749)

Neyelov, Vasily Ivanovich (1722–82) (s.v. Neyelov)

Nymphenburg, Schloss (s.v. Munich IV. Buildings. 3. Schloss Nymphenburg)

Office of Works

Olivares, Conde-Duque de [Guzmán y Pimentel, Gaspar de; Olivares, 3rd Conde de] (1587–1645)

Osuna, Duquesa de Osuna [María Josefa de la Soledad Alonso Pimental; Condesa de Benavente] (1752–1834) (s.v. Osuna (3) Duquesa de Osuna)

Painshill Park

Palissy, Bernard (1510–90)

Palladio, Andrea (1508–80)

Paul I [Pavel Petrovich], Emperor of Russia (1754–1801) (s.v. Romanov (4))

Pavilion

Peter I [Peter the Great], Tsar and Emperor of Russia (1672–1725) (s.v. Romanov (1))

Peterhof

Philip II, King of Spain (1527–98) (s.v. Habsburg, §II (2))

Philip IV, King of Spain (1605–65) (s.v. Habsburg, §II (7))

Piper, Fredrik Magnus (1746–1824)

Pitt, Thomas, 1st Baron Camelford (1737–93)

Pope, Alexander (1688–1744)

Pushkin [Tsarskoye Selo] (Yekaterininsky Palace)

Rastrelli, Bartolomeo Francesco (1700–71)

Roberts, Thomas Sautell (1760–1826)

Rousseau, Jean-Jacques (1712–78)

Rysbrack, Michael (1694–1770)

Sadeler, Jan [Johan] I (1550–1600)
Sadeler, Raphael I (1560/61–1628/32)
Sandby, Thomas (1721–98)
Sandoval y Rojas, Francisco Gómez de, Duque de Lerma (1552–1625)
Schloss Nymphenburg, *see* Nymphenburg, Schloss
Sckell, Friedrich Ludwig von (1750–1823)
Sheremet'yev, Pyotr (Borisovich), Count (1713–87)
Sporck [Špork], Franz Anton [František Antonín], Graf von (1662–1738)
Stourhead
Stuart, James [Athenian] (1713–88)
Stukeley, William (1687–1765)
Versailles
Vignola, Jacopo (1507–73)
Vos, Marten de, the elder (1532–1603)
Walpole, Horace [Horatio] William, fourth earl of Orford (1717–97)
Wilhelmshöhe (s.v. Kassel (3) Wilhelmshöhe)
Winter Palace [Zimni Dvorets; now part of the Hermitage Museum]
  (s.v. St Petersburg IV. Buildings (1))
Wood, John (bap. 1704, d. 1754)
Wörlitz
Wyatt, James (1746–1813)
Wyatt, Samuel (1737–1807)
Yuste Monastery

Oxford Dictionary of National Biography

Acland, Sir Thomas Dyke, tenth baronet (1787–1871)
Adam, Robert (1728–92)
Aislabie, John (1670–1742)
Amhurst, Nicholas (1697–1742)
Augusta Sophia, Princess (1768–1840) (s.v. George III, daughters of)
Bacon, Francis, Viscount St Alban (1561–1626)
Bathurst, Allen, first Earl Bathurst (1684–1775)
Battie, William (bap. 1703, d. 1776)
Beckford, William Thomas (1760–1844)
Boothby, Sir Brooke, seventh baronet (1744–1824)
Boulton, Matthew (1728–1809)
Bowles, William Lisle (1762–1850)
Boyle, John, fifth earl of Cork and fifth earl of Orrery (1707–62)

Boyle, Richard, third earl of Burlington and fourth earl of Cork (1694–1753)

Boyle, Robert (1627–91)

Brewer, James Norris (*fl.* 1799–1830)

Bridgeman [Bridgman], Charles (d. 1738)

Brown, Lancelot [known as Capability Brown] (1716–83)

Browne, Thomas, fourth Viscount Kenmare (1726–95)

Burns, Robert (1759–96)

Bushell, Thomas (b. before 1600, d. 1674)

Byng, John (bap. 1704, d. 1757)

Byng, John, fifth Viscount Torrington (1743–1813)

Byron, George Gordon Noel, sixth Baron Byron (1788–1824)

Caroline, Queen (1768–1821), consort of George IV

Campbell, Colen, of Boghole and Urchany (1676–1729)

Campbell, John, third earl of Breadalbane and Holland (bap. 1696, d. 1782)

Campbell, John, second marquess of Breadalbane (1796–1862)

Castle, Richard (d. 1751)

Caulfeild, James, first earl of Charlemont (1728–99)

Cecil, Robert, first earl of Salisbury (1563–1612)

Cecil, William, first Baron Burghley (1520/21–1598)

Chambers, Sir William (1722–96)

Charlotte, Queen (1744–1818), consort of George III

Clarke, Samuel (1675–1729)

Cooper, Anthony Ashley, third earl of Shaftesbury (1671–1713)

Cowper, William (1731–1800)

Crisp, Sir Frank, first baronet (1843–1919)

Curll, Edmund (d. 1747)

Curzon, Nathaniel, first Baron Scarsdale (1726–1804)

Darwin, Erasmus (1731–1802)

Dashwood, Francis, eleventh Baron Le Despencer (1708–81)

Delany, Mary (1700–88)

Dodsley, Robert (1704–64)

Duck, Stephen (1705?–1756)

Elizabeth [née Lady Elizabeth Berkeley], margravine of Brandenburg-Ansbach-Bayreuth [other married name Elizabeth Craven, Lady Craven] (1750–1828)

Elizabeth, Princess (1770–1840), landgravine of Hesse-Homburg, consort of Friedrich VI (s.v. George III, daughters of)

Evelyn, John (1620–1706)

Fane, John, seventh earl of Westmorland (bap. 1686, d. 1762)

Finch, George, ninth earl of Winchilsea and fourth earl of Nottingham (1752–1826) (s.v. White Conduit cricket club)

Finlay, Ian Hamilton (1925–2006)

Fisher, Jonathan (d. 1809)

Flitcroft, Henry (1697–1769)

Foster, John, first Baron Oriel (1740–1828)

Franciscans [Monks of Medmenham] (active c.1750–c.1776)

Frederick Lewis, Prince of Wales (1707–51)

Fuller, John (1757–1834)

Gilbert [formerly Giddy], Davies (1767–1839) [written without knowledge of the Gilbert archive at East Sussex Record Office]

Gilpin, William (1724–1804)

Goldsmith, Oliver (1728?–1774)

Graham, James Gillespie (1776–1855)

Granville, George, Baron Lansdowne and Jacobite duke of Albemarle (1666–1735)

Graves, Richard (1715–1804)

Grenville [later Grenville-Temple], Richard, second Earl Temple (1711–79)

Guy of Warwick (supposedly fl. c.930)

Hamilton, Charles (1704–68)

Hamilton, James, sixth earl of Abercorn (c.1661–1734)

Hanbury, John (1664?–1734)

Hardinge, Nicholas (1699–1758)

Harrison, George (1943–2001)

Hill, David Octavius (1802–70)

Hill, Richard (1655/6–1727)

Hill, Sir Richard, second baronet (1733–1808)

Hill, Sir Rowland (c.1495–1561)

Hoare, Henry (1705–85)

Hobday, William Armfield (1771–1831)

Hogg, James (bap. 1770, d. 1835)

Hollins, William (1763–1843)

Isham, Sir Charles Edmund, tenth baronet (1819–1903)

Jago, Richard (1715–81)

Jefferson, Thomas (1743–1826)

Jelfe, Andrews (c.1690–1759)

John of Beverley [St John of Beverley] (d. 721), bishop of York

Johnson, Esther [Stella] (1681–1728)

Johnson, Samuel (1709 84)

Keene, Henry (1726–76)

Kent, William (1686–1748)

Knight [née St John], Henrietta, Lady Luxborough (1699–1756)

Knight, Richard Payne (1751–1824)

Langley, Batty (1696–1751)

Lee, Sir Henry (1533–1611)

Lennox, Charles, first duke of Richmond, first duke of Lennox, and duke of Aubigny in the French nobility (1672–1723)

Lennox, Charles, second duke of Richmond, second duke of Lennox, and duke of Aubigny (1701–50)

Locke, John (1632–1704)

Loveday, John (1711–89)

Lunar Society of Birmingham (active c.1765–c.1800)

Luttrell, Henry Lawes, second earl of Carhampton (1737–1821)

Lyttelton, George, first Baron Lyttelton (1709–73)

MacCarthy, Denis Florence (1817–82)

Macpherson, James (1736–96)

Madan [née Cowper], Judith (1702–81)

Mary, Queen (1867–1953), consort of George V

Mason, William (1725–97)

Mead, Richard (1673–1754)

Miller, Sanderson (1716–80)

Montagu, George, fourth duke of Manchester (1737–88)

Montagu, Lady Mary Wortley [née Lady Mary Pierrepont] (bap. 1689, d. 1762)

Morris, Roger (1695–1749)

Murray, James, second duke of Atholl (1690–1764)

Newton, Sir Isaac (1642–1727)

Oates, Lawrence Edward Grace (1880–1912)

Parnell, Sir John, second baronet (1745–1801)

Parnell, Thomas (1679–1718)

Pearse, Patrick Henry (1879–1916)

Perceval, John, first earl of Egmont (1683–1748)

Percy, Thomas (1729–1811)

Pitt, Thomas, first Baron Camelford (1737–93)

Pococke, Richard (1704–65)

Polwhele, Richard (1760–1838)

Pope, Alexander (1688–1744)

Priestley, Joseph (1733–1804)
Pryme, Abraham (1671–1704)
Quin, Michael Joseph (1796–1843)
Radcliffe, John (bap. 1650, d. 1714)
Riddell, Robert, of Glenriddell (bap. 1755, d. 1794)
Roberts, Thomas Sautelle (1760?–1826) (s.n. Roberts, Thomas)
Robinson [née Darby], Mary [Perdita] (1756/1758?–1800)
Rogers, Samuel (1763–1855)
Rolle, John, Baron Rolle (bap. 1751, d. 1842)
Rysbrack, (John) Michael (1694–1770)
St John, Henry, first Viscount Bolingbroke (1678–1751)
Sandby, Thomas (1721–98)
Sandby, Thomas (bap. 1723, d. 1798)
Scott, Henry, third duke of Buccleuch and fifth duke of Queensberry
    (1746–1812)
Seymour [née Thynne], Frances, duchess of Somerset (1699–1754)
Shenstone, William (1714–63)
Sheridan, Thomas (1719?–1788)
Sitwell, Dame Edith Louisa (1887–1964)
Sitwell, Sir (Francis) Osbert Sacheverell, fifth baronet (1892–1969)
Skeffington, Clotworthy, second earl of Massereene (1742–1805)
Smith, Albert Richard (1816–60)
Soane, Sir John (1753–1837)
Somerset, Charles Noel, fourth duke of Beaufort (1709–56) (s.n. Somerset,
    Henry, second duke of Beaufort)
Somervile [Somerville], William (1675–1742)
Stuart, James [called Athenian Stuart] (1713–88)
Stukeley, William (1687–1765)
Swete [formerly Tripe], John (1752–1821)
Swithun [St Swithun] (d. 863)
Temple, Richard, first Viscount Cobham (1675–1749)
Thackeray, William Makepeace (1811–63)
Thicknesse, Philip (1719–92)
Timbs, John (1801–75)
Tusser, Thomas (c.1524–1580)
Unwin [née Cawthorne], Mary (bap. 1723, d. 1796)
Veitch, John (1752–1839) [s.v. Veitch family]
Walford, Thomas (1752–1833)

Walpole, Horatio [Horace], fourth earl of Orford (1717–97)

Walter, Henry (1785–1859)

Warton, Thomas (1728–90)

Watt, James (1736–1819)

Webbe, Samuel, the elder (1740–1816)

Wedgwood, Josiah (1730–95)

West, Gilbert (1703–56)

Wharton, Philip James, duke of Wharton and Jacobite duke of Northumberland (1698–1731)

Whately, Thomas (1726–72)

White, Gilbert (1720–93)

Wilkes, John (1725–97)

William Augustus, Prince, duke of Cumberland (1721–65)

Wilson, John [pseudonym: Christopher North] (1785–1854)

Wollaston, William (1659–1724)

Wood, John (bap. 1704, d. 1754)

Wright, Thomas (1711–86)

Wyatt, James (1746–1813)

Wyatt, Samuel (1737–1807)

Wyatt, Thomas Henry (1807–80)

Wyndham, Sir Hugh (1602/3–1684)

Yates, Edmund Hodgson (1831–94)

Yorke [née Campbell], Jemima, *suo jure* Marchioness Grey (1722–97)

Yorke, Philip, first earl of Hardwicke (1690–1764)

Yorke, Philip, second earl of Hardwicke (1720–90)

Yorke, Philip, third earl of Hardwicke (1757–1834)

Manuscripts, and Images not reproduced in the text

BIRMINGHAM MUSEUM AND ART GALLERY

John Phillp, pen-and-ink drawing of Soho hermitage (BM&AG 2003 0031 11 (16/6997))

John Phillp, pen-and-ink drawing with watercolour of Soho hermitage in snow (BM&AG 2003 0031 17 (16/7017))

Portrait of James Guidney (BM&AG 1932V138.2)

EAST SUSSEX RECORD OFFICE, LEWES

Inventory of Gildredge estate (1816) (GIL 4/39/4)

Colour-wash picture of Eastbourne hermitage (GIL 4/36/2)

ESSEX RECORD OFFICE

Drawing of Hermitage in Whitley Wood (I/Mp 37/1/1); image available on-line

LONDON SCHOOL OF ECONOMICS

Sir John Parnell, 'Journal of a Tour throu' Wales and England Anno 1769' (MS Coll Misc 38)

NATIONAL LIBRARY OF WALES

Thomas Martyn, 'A tour to south Wales etc. 1801' (NLW MS 1340C); image available on-line

SHROPSHIRE ARCHIVES, SHREWSBURY

John Homes Smith, Watercolour of the Hermitage, Tong, dated 21 May 1822 (6009/339 (235/13106)); image available on-line
John Homes Smith, Watercolour of the Hermitage, Tong (6009/338 (235/13105)); image available on-line
Photograph of the hermit in his cell at Hawkstone (PC/G/1-PC/H/29 (251/14964)); image available on-line

VICTORIA AND ALBERT MUSEUM, LONDON

Sketch of hermitage at Lilliput Castle (2006AA3578)

Books, Journals, and Articles

Adams, William Howard, *The French Garden 1500–1800* (London and New York, 1979).
Andrews, Malcolm, *The Search for the Picturesque: Landscape Aesthetics and Tourism in Britain, 1760–1800* (London, 1989).
Anon [William Gilpin?], *Stow: the gardens of the Right Honourable the Lord Viscount Cobham. Containing, I. Forty views of the temples and other ornamental buildings … II. A description of all the buildings … III. A dialogue upon the said gardens* (London, 1750).
Anon, 'Memoir of William Armfield Hobday', *Arnold's Library of Fine Arts*, 11/2 (London, 1831).
Anon, *A New Description of Sir John Soane's Museum* (London, 1955; 11th rev. edn., 2007).
Atkinson, A., *Ireland exhibited to England in a political and moral survey of her population, and in a statistical and scenographic tour of certain districts,*

comprehending specimens of her colonisation, natural history and antiquities, arts, sciences, and commerce, customs, character, and manners, seats, scenes and sea views, 2 vols. (London, 1823).

Auden, John Ernest, *Notes on the History of Tong*, from the parish books, ed. Joyce Frost, 2 vols. (vol. 2, Bury St Edmunds, 2007).

Balderston, Gordon, 'Giovanni Battista Guelfi: Five Busts for Queen Caroline's Hermitage in Richmond', *Sculpture Journal* 17 (2008), 83–8.

Barre, Dianne, 'Sir Samuel Hellier (1736–84) and his Garden Buildings: Part of the Midlands "Garden Circuit" in the 1760s–70s?', *Garden History* 36 (2008), 310–27.

Batey, Mavis, 'Nuneham Courtenay: An Oxfordshire Eighteenth-Century Deserted Village', *Oxoniensa* 33 (1968), 108–24.

Batey, Mavis, 'Oliver Goldsmith: An Indictment of Landscape Gardening', in Peter Willis (ed.), *Furor Hortensis: Essays on the History of the English Landscape Garden in Memory of H. F. Clark* (Edinburgh, 1974), 57–71.

Batey, Mavis, *Jane Austen and the English Landscape* (London, 1996).

Belfast Monthly Magazine 3 (July–December 1809).

Bickham, George, *The Beauties of Stow, or a Description of the most noble house, gardens and magnificent buildings therein, with above thirty copper plates ... two views of the house, and a curious general plan of the whole gardens* (3rd edn., London, 1753) [contains Gilbert West's 'Stowe, a poem'].

Brown, Jonathan, and Elliott, John H., *A Palace for a King: The Buen Retiro and the Court of Philip IV* (revised and expanded edn., New Haven, 2004).

Brown, M. E., *A Man of No Taste Whatsoever: Joseph Pocklington, 1736–1817* (privately printed, 2010).

Bushell, Thomas, *The first part of youths errors. Written by Thomas Bushel, the superlative prodigall* (London, 1628).

Byng, John, *The Torrington diaries, containing the tours through England and Wales of the Hon. John Byng (later fifth Viscount Torrington) between the years 1781 and 1794*, ed. C. Bruyn Andrews, 4 vols. (London, 1934–8).

Calder, Martin, 'Promenade in Ermenonville', in Martin Calder (ed.), *Experiencing the Garden in the Eighteenth Century* (Bern, 2006), 109–44.

Chambers, Robert, *The Book of Days: A Miscellany of Popular Antiquities*, 2 vols. (London, 1862–4).

Cloake, John, *Palaces and Parks of Richmond and Kew. Vol. 2: Richmond Lodge and the Kew Palaces* (Chichester, 1996).

Coke, David, and Borg, Alan, *Vauxhall Gardens: A History* (New Haven and London, 2011).

Colegate, Isabel, *A Pelican in the Wilderness: Hermits, Solitaries and Recluses* (London, 2002).

Colton, Judith, 'Kent's Hermitage for Queen Caroline at Richmond', *Architectura* 2 (1974), 181–91.

Cork, The Countess of (ed.), *The Orrery Papers*, 2 vols. (London, 1903).

Cornforth, John, 'Where Fishes Fly', *Country Life* (5 May 1988), 166–7 [on the new grotto at Leeds Castle].

Courier no. 4582 (11 January 1810).

Craftsman no. 491 (13 September 1735).

Curll, Edmund, *The Rarities of Richmond: being exact descriptions of the Royal Hermitage and Merlin's Cave with his life and prophecies* (2nd edn., London, 1736).

Curwen, J. F., 'Some Notes on the Hermitage at Conishead Priory, Lancashire', *Transactions of the Cumberland and Westmorland Antiquarian and Archaeological Society* NS 3 (1903), 72–7.

Decker, Paul, *Gothic Architecture decorated: consisting of a large collection of temples, banqueting, summer and green houses; gazebo's, alcoves; faced, garden and umbrello'd seats… &c.,…: likewise designs of the Gothic orders, with their proper ornaments, and rules for drawing them*, 2 vols. (London, 1759; facsimile edn., Farnborough, Hants, 1968).

Delany, Mary, *The autobiography and correspondence of Mary Granville, Mrs Delany: with… reminiscences of King George the third & Queen Charlotte*, ed. Lady Llanover, 3 vols. (London, 1861); 2nd series, 3 vols. (1862).

Dezallier d'Argenville, Antoine-Nicolas, *Voyage pittoresque des environs de Paris* (1792).

Dixon, Anne Campbell, 'Hermits for Hire', *Country Life* (2 June 1988), 160–3.

Dodsley, Robert, 'A Description of The Leasowes', in R. Dodsley (ed.), *The Works in Verse and Prose of William Shenstone*, 2 vols. (London, 1764), ii. 333–71.

Douglas, Anna, 'Solitude: The Hermit Project', *Follies Journal* 3 (2003), 17–27.

Du Cerceau, Jacques Androuet, *Le Premier Volume des plus excellent bastiments de France*, actually in 2 vols. (Paris, 1576–9; facsimile reprint, Farnborough, 1988).

Dugdale, James, *The New British Traveller, or Modern Panorama of England and Wales*, 4 vols. (London, 1819).

Egleton, Margaret, *Gnomeland: An Introduction to the Little People* (London, 2007).

Evelyn, John, *Elysium Britannicum, or the Royal Gardens*, ed. John Ingram (Philadelphia, 2000).

Fisher, Jonathan, *Scenery of Ireland: illustrated in a series of prints of select views, castles and abbies, drawn and engraved in aquatinta, volume the first containing sixty prints with a letter press description to each* (London and Dublin, 1795).

Fitzell, John, *The Hermit in German Literature, from Lessing to Eichendorff* (Chapel Hill, NC, 1961).

Fitzgerald, Olda, *Irish Gardens* (London, 1999).

'Florence' [Denis Florence MacCarthy?], 'Hermits, Ornamental and Experimental', *Notes and Queries* 5, no. 119 (7 February 1852), 123–4.

Freeman, Daniel, *The Opera Theater of Count von Sporck in Prague* (Hillsdale, NY, 1992).

Gell, Sir William, *A Tour in the Lakes made in 1797*, ed. William Rollinson (Newcastle-upon-Tyne, 1968).

Gentleman's Magazine (April 1733, 30 June 1735, 21 August 1735, 13 September 1735, September 1814, October 1822).

Girouard, Mark, *Life in the English Country House: A Social and Architectural History* (New Haven, 1978).

Gothein, Marie Luise, *Geschichte der Gartenkunst*, 2 vols. (1914), trans. as *A History of Garden Art*, ed. Walter P. Wright, trans. Mrs Archer-Hind, 2 vols. (London and Toronto, 1928; reprinted 1966).

Granville, George (Lord Lansdowne), *The British Enchanters: or, no magick like love. A tragedy* (London, 1706).

Graves, Richard, *Columella, or, The Distressed Anchoret, a colloquial tale* (London, 1779; reprinted Toulouse, 1989).

Griffiths, George, *A history of Tong, Shropshire, its church, manor, parish, college, early owners, and clergy, with notes on Boscobel* (Newport, Salop, 1894).

Guidney, James, *Some particulars of the life and adventures of James Guidney, a well-known character in Birmingham, written from his own account of himself* (3rd and enlarged edn., Birmingham, 1862).

Halfpenny, William and John, *The Country gentleman's pocket companion and builder's assistant, for rural decorative architecture: containing 32 new designs, plans, and elevations of alcoves, floats, temples, summer-houses, lodges, huts, grotto's, etc. in the Augustine, Gothick and Chinese taste, with proper directions annexed; also an exact estimate of their several amounts, which are from 25 to 100 pounds, and most of them portable* (London, 1753).

Hammond, [Lieutenant], 'A Relation of a Short Survey of the Western Counties Made by a Lieutenant of the Military Company in Norwich in 1635', in *Camden Miscellany*, 3rd series, 52 (1936), 1–128.

[Hanway, Mary Ann], *A Journey to the Highlands of Scotland, with occasional remarks on Dr Johnson's Tour* (London, n.d. [*c*.1776]).

Harris, Eileen, 'The Architecture of Thomas Wright', *Country Life* (Part I, 29 August 1971, pp. 492–5; Part 2, 2 September 1971, pp. 546–50; Part 3, 9 September 1971, pp. 612–50).

Harris, Eileen, 'Hunting for Hermits', *Country Life* (26 May 1988), 186–9.

Harris, Leslie, *Robert Adam and Kedleston: The Making of a Neo-Classical Masterpiece*, ed. Gervase Jackson-Stops ([London], 1987).

Harwood, Edward S., 'Luxurious Hermits: Asceticism, Luxury and Retirement in the Eighteenth-Century English Garden', in *Studies in the History of Gardens and Designed Landscapes* 20 (2000), 265–96.

Haycock, David Boyd, *William Stukeley: Science, Archaeology and Religion in Eighteenth-Century England* (Woodbridge, Suffolk, 2002).

Headley, Gwyn, and Meulenkamp, Wim, *Follies: A National Trust Guide* (London, 1986; rev. edn., 1990).

Heaney, Seamus, *Station Island* (London, 1984).

Heely, Joseph, *A description of Hagley, Envil and the Leasowes, wherein all the Latin inscriptions are translated, and every particular beauty described. Interspersed with Critical Observations* (Birmingham, [1775?]).

Heely, Joseph, *A description of the Leasowes. By the author of Letters on the beauties of Hagley, Envil, and the Leasowes* (London, 1777).

Heely, Joseph, *Letters on the beauties of Hagley, Envil, and the Leasowes. With critical remarks and observations on the modern taste in gardening*, 2 vols. (London, 1777).

Hoare, Sir Richard Colt, *The Journeys of Sir Richard Colt Hoare through Wales and England, 1793–1810*, ed. M. W. Thompson (Gloucester, 1983).

Holt-White, Rashleigh, *The Life and Letters of Gilbert White of Selborne*, 2 vols. (London, 1901).

Horn, Walter, Marshall, Jenny White, and Rourke, Grellan D., *The Forgotten Hermitage of Skellig Michael* (Berkeley, Los Angeles, and Oxford, 1990).

Howley, James, *The Follies and Garden Buildings of Ireland* (New Haven, 1993).

Hull, Thomas (ed.), *Select Letters between the late Duchess of Somerset, Lady Luxborough, Miss Dolman, Mr Whistler, Mr R. Dodsley, William Shenstone Esq. and others*, 2 vols. (London, 1778).

Hunt, John Dixon, 'A Silent and Solitary Hermitage', *Annual Report of the York Georgian Society* (1970), 47–60.

Hunt, John Dixon, *William Kent, Landscape Garden Designer: An Assessment and Catalogue of his Designs* (London, 1987).

Hutchinson, Geoff, *Fuller of Sussex: A Georgian Squire* (Brede, East Sussex, 1993; rev. edn., 1997).

Innes, Michael [J. I. M. Stewart], *Stop Press* (London, 1939).

Jackson, Mick, 'Hermit Wanted', in *Ten Sorry Tales* (London, 2006).

Jeffery, Robert, *Discovering Tong: Its History, Myths and Curiosities* (Tong, 2007).

Johnson, Samuel, 'Shenstone', *Lives of the English Poets*, ed. G. B. Hill, 3 vols. (1905), iii. 348–60.

Jones, Barbara, *Follies and Grottoes* (London, 1953; rev. and enlarged edn., 1974).

Kempelen, Wolfgang von, *Le Mécanisme de la parole, suivi de la description d'une machine parlante* (Vienna, 1791).

Laird, Mark, and Weisberg-Roberts, Alicia, *Mrs Delany and her Circle* (New Haven and London, 2009).

Langley, Batty, *Gothic Architecture improved by rules and proportions: In many grand designs of columns, doors, windows, chimney-pieces, arcades, colonades, porticos, umbrellos, temples, and pavillions &c.: With plans, elevations and profiles geometrically explained: To which is added an historical dissertation on Gothic architecture* (London, 1742).

Le Rouge, Georges-Louis, *Détail des nouveaux jardins à la mode*, ed. Iris Lauterbach (Nördlingen, 2009). Veröffentlichungen des Zentralinstituts für Kunstgeschichte in München, Band XXIII ['Réimpression de l'édition originale Paris 1775–90'].

Luxborough, Lady, *Letters written by the late Right Honourable Lady Luxborough to William Shenstone, Esq* (London, 1775).

McCann, T. J., '"Much troubled with very rude company...", The 2nd Duke of Richmond's Menagerie at Goodwood', *Sussex Archaeological Collections* 132 (1994), 143–9.

Malcomson, A. P. W., 'Election Politics in the Borough of Antrim, 1750–1800', *Irish Historical Studies* 17 (1970), 32–57 [on the Thompsons of Greenmount].

Malins, Edward Greenway, and the Knight of Glin, *Lost Demesnes: Irish Landscape Gardening, 1660–1845* (London, 1976).

Markham, Sarah, *John Loveday of Caversham, 1711–1789: The Life and Tours of an Eighteenth-Century Onlooker* (Wilton, Salisbury, Wiltshire, 1984).

Martin, Peter, *Pursuing Innocent Pleasures: The Gardening World of Alexander Pope* (London, 1984).

Miller, Naomi, *Heavenly Caves: Reflections on the Garden Grotto* (New York, 1982).

Moore, Lisa Lynne, 'Queer Gardens: Mary Delany's Flowers and Friendships', *Eighteenth-Century Studies* 39 (2005), 49–70.

Mowl, Tim, and Earnshaw, Brian, *Trumpet at a Distant Gate: The Lodge as a Prelude to the Country House* (London, 1985).

Mowl, Timothy, and Barre, Dianne, *The Historic Gardens of Staffordshire* (Bristol, 2009).

North, Christopher, 'Noctes Ambrosianae' No. 48, *Blackwood's Edinburgh Magazine* 27 (April 1830), 659–94.

Pattison, Paul, 'Oldstone: A Mansion and its Gardens in South Devon: A Survey by the Royal Commission on the Historical Monuments of England', *Proceedings of the Devon Archaeological Society* 50 (1992), 125–36.

Piggott, Stuart, *The Druids* (Harmondsworth, 1974).

Piggott, Stuart, *William Stukeley: An Eighteenth-Century Antiquary* (London, 1950; rev. and enlarged edn., 1985).

Pryme, Abraham de la, *Memoirs of Thomas Bushell*, ed. William Harrison, Publications of the Manx Society, vol. 30 (Douglas, 1878).

Pückler-Muskau, Prince Hermann von, *Tour in England, Ireland, and France in the years 1826, 1827, 1828 and 1829 ... by a German Prince* (Philadelphia, 1833) [translation of *Briefes Eines Verstorbenen* ('Letters from a dead man') by Sarah Austin].

Pyne, William Henry, *The history of the royal residences of Windsor Castle, St. James's Palace, Carlton House, Kensington Palace, Hampton Court, Buckingham House, and Frogmore*, 3 vols. (London, 1819).

Radcliffe, David Hill, 'Genre and Social Order in Country House Poems of the Eighteenth Century: Four Views of Percy Lodge', *Studies in English Literature* 30 (1990), 445–65.

Riskin, Jessica, 'The Defecating Duck, or, the Ambiguous Origins of Artificial Life', *Critical Inquiry* 29 (2003), 599–633.

Roden, Earl of (ed.), *The Diaries of Lord Limerick's Grand Tour, 1716 to 1723* ([Cashel, Co. Tipperary], 2005); reprinted from *County Louth Archaeological and Historical Journal* 23 (2003).

Roden, Earl of, *Tollymore: The Story of an Irish Desmesne* (Belfast, 2005).

Rogers, Samuel, *Recollections of the Table Talk of Samuel Rogers* (3rd edn., London, 1856).

Ross, Stephanie, *What Gardens Mean* (Chicago, 1998).

Rousseau, Jean-Jacques, *Julie, ou la nouvelle Héloïse* (Amsterdam, 1761); translated into English as *Eloisa: Or, a series of original letters collected and published by J. J. Rousseau*, 4 vols. (London, 1769).

Rykwert, Joseph, *On Adam's House in Paradise: The Idea of the Primitive Hut in Architectural Theory* (New York, 1972).

Sadeler, Johan I and Raphael, *Solitudo, sive vitae partum eremicolarum*, in *The Illustrated Bartsch: Johan I Sadeler*, vol. 70, Part 2, ed. Isabelle De Ramaix (Norwalk, Conn., 2001), 169–219 (engravings 348–77, mostly after drawings by Marten de Vos).

Sambrook, James, 'Painshill Park in the 1760's', *Garden History* 8 (1980), 91–106.

Schlesinger, Max, *Saunterings in and about London* (London, 1853).

Sicca, Cinzia Maria, 'Like a Shallow Cave by Nature Made: William Kent's "Natural" Architecture at Richmond', *Architectura* 16 (1986), 68–82.

Sirén, Osvald, *China and Gardens of Europe of the Eighteenth Century* (New York, 1950).

Sitwell, Edith, *English Eccentrics* (London, 1933).

Sitwell, Osbert, 'A German Eighteenth-Century Town', *Criterion* 2/8 (July 1924), 433–47.

Smiles, Sam, *The Image of Antiquity: Ancient Britain and the Romantic Imagination* (New Haven, 1994).

Soane, John, *Description of the house and museum on the north side of Lincoln's Inn Fields: the residence of John Soane, Architect* (London, 1830; expanded 2nd edn., 1835).

Spence, Cathryn, 'For True Friends: Jerry Peirce's Patriot Whig Garden at Lilliput Castle', *Bath History* 12 (2011), 20–41.

Stafford, Fiona, *The Sublime Savage: James Macpherson and the Poems of Ossian* (Edinburgh, 1988).

Stamper, Paul, 'Of Naked Venuses and Drunken Bacchanals: The Durants of Tong Castle, Shropshire', in Michael Costen (ed.), *People and Places: Essays in Honour of Mick Aston* (Oxford, 2007), 181–94.

Stillenau, Gottwald Caesar von, *Leben…Grafen von Sporck* (n.p. [Prague or Amsterdam?], 1720).

Stoppard, Tom, *Arcadia* (London, 1993).

Stukeley, William, *Abury, a Temple of the British Druids* (London, 1743).

Stukeley, William, *Stonehenge, a Temple Restor'd to the British Druids* (London, 1740).

Swift, Jonathan, *Poems*, ed. Harold Williams, 3 vols. (Oxford, 1937; 2nd edn., 1958).

Symes, Michael, *Mr Hamilton's Elysium: The Gardens of Painshill* (London, 2010).

Symes, Michael, and Haynes, Sandy, *Enville, Hagley, The Leasowes: Three Great Eighteenth-Century Gardens* (Bristol, 2010).

Taylor, Patrick (ed.), *The Oxford Companion to the Garden* (Oxford, 2006).

Temple, Nigel, 'A Hermit for Cadland?: "the soner the better"', *Follies Journal* 3 (2003), 3–16.

Thacker, Christopher, *The History of Gardens* (London, 1979; reprinted Beckenham, 1985).

Thacker, Christopher, 'An Extraordinary Solitude', in Sandra Raphael *et al.* (eds.), *Of Oxfordshire Gardens* (Oxford, 1982), 26–48.

Thicknesse, Philip, *Memoirs and anecdotes of Philip Thicknesse, late governor of Landguard Fort, and unfortunately father to George Touchet, Baron Audley*, 3 vols. (Dublin; 2 vols. in 1788, vol. 3 in 1791).

Timbs, John, *English Eccentrics and Eccentricities* (London, 1875).

Victoria, Queen, *Highland Journals*, ed. David Duff (Exeter, 1980).

Walpole, Horace, *The History of the Modern Taste in Gardening*, ed. John Dixon Hunt (New York, 1982).

Whately, Thomas, *Observations on Modern Gardening* (Dublin, 1770).

White, Gilbert, *The Natural History of Selborne* (Oxford, 2012).

White, Henry, *The Diaries of an 18th Century Parson: Rev. Henry White, Rector of Fyfield, Andover, Hampshire*, ed. Clive Burton (Andover, 1979).

White, Roger (ed.), *Georgian Arcadia* (London, 1987).

Wilton-Ely, John, 'The Genesis and Evolution of Fonthill Abbey', *Architectural History* 23 (1980), 40–51.

Woodbridge, Kenneth, *Landscape and Antiquity: Aspects of English Culture at Stourhead, 1718 to 1838* (Oxford, 1970).

Wordsworth, Dorothy, *Recollections of a Tour Made in Scotland, A.D. 1803* (1874).

Wright, Thomas, *Arbours & grottoes: a facsimile of the two parts of Universal architecture (1755 and 1758), with a catalogue of Wright's works in architecture and garden design by Eileen Harris* (London, 1979).

Wrighte, William, *Grotesque Architecture Or Rural Amusement: Consisting Of Plans, Elevations, And Sections For Huts, Retreats, Summer And Winter Hermitages, Terminaries, Chinese, Gothic and Natural Grottoes, Cascades, Baths, Mosques, Moresque Pavilions, Grotesque and Rustic Seats, Green Houses etc. Many of which may be executed with Flints, Irregular Stones, Rude Branches, and Roots of Trees* (London, 1767) [1790 edition reprinted in facsimile, 2010].

Yates, Edmund Hodgson, *Edmund Yates, his Recollections and Experiences* (4th edn., London, 1885).

PICTURE ACKNOWLEDGEMENTS

INDEX

Note: Reference to figures are in italics